The
Gatling Gun

The
Gatling Gun

19th Century Machine Gun to 21st Century Vulcan

Joseph Berk

PALADIN PRESS
BOULDER, COLORADO

The Gatling Gun:
19th Century Machine Gun to 21st Century Vulcan
by Joseph Berk

Copyright © 1991 by Joseph Berk

ISBN 0-87364-644-4
Printed in the United States of America

Library of Congress Catalog Card Number: 91-50795

Published by Paladin Press, a division of
Paladin Enterprises, Inc., P.O. Box 1307,
Boulder, Colorado 80306, USA.
(303) 443-7250

Direct inquires and/or orders to the above address.

Neither the author nor the publisher assumes

CONTENTS

V

This book is dedicated to the girls . . . Susan, Lauren, and Erica.

CHAPTER 1

Richard Jordan Gatling

Richard Jordan Gatling was born to Jordan and Mary Gatling on the family plantation in North Carolina on 12 September 1818. The new Gatling baby was fortunate, for he had been born to one of the wealthiest families in the area, and his father was a man of above-average intellect and mechanical aptitude. In addition to prospering as a farmer and landowner, Jordan Gatling, a man of self-made wealth, was also a master blacksmith and carpenter. Watching him work endowed young Richard with an appreciation for mechanisms and fine workmanship. Spending the first twenty-six years of his life on and around the family plantation allowed Richard not only to attend the Buckhorn Academy (one of the better schools in rural North Carolina), but to gain an appreciation for how machinery might ease man's burden.

Richard's aptitude for invention surfaced in 1835, when he was seventeen years old. While in Virginia on family business, he observed U.S. Navy tests of several new ship-propulsion concepts, none of which were successful. His mind went to work on the problem, and he created a screw-propeller concept. Unfortunately, a Swede named John Ericcson had the same idea and secured a patent before Gatling could. (Ericcson became wealthy as a result and went on to build the world's first ironclad warship, the *Monitor*.)

Gatling's Early Success

Undaunted, Gatling patented both the concept and a detailed design for a rice planting machine in 1839. (Having learned from his loss on the screw propeller, Gatling developed a lifelong pattern of patenting all ideas immediately.)

In 1844, Gatling moved to St. Louis, where he spent the next three years. He began to manufacture and market his planting machine in 1845 and became a wealthy man. On one of his marketing trips during the winter of 1845-1846, Gatling contracted smallpox and nearly died. During his lengthy recovery, he no doubt spent a good deal of time pondering the deficiencies of mid-nineteenth century medicine. (He had already lost two of his younger sisters to disease when he became ill; the third died shortly after his recovery.)

Medical School

These events probably combined to kindle Gatling's interest in medicine. At the age of twenty-nine, he was a wealthy man who could do almost anything he desired. He decided to study medicine, attending both Indiana Medical College and Ohio Medical College over a period of two and one-half years. No evidence exists to verify that Gatling earned a degree in medicine or ever practiced. Nonetheless, he always used the title "Doctor" after leaving Ohio Medical College.

More Inventions

Gatling's propensity for invention had continued to manifest itself while he studied medicine. When he neared completion of his studies at Ohio Medical College in late 1849, he attempted to patent a compressed air distribution system. Although the U.S. Patent Office disapproved his patent request, claiming that the concept did not qualify as an invention, Gatling developed a lifelong interest in the applications of compressed air and steam. Many of his subsequent inventions utilized one or the other.

The Indianapolis Years

After leaving Ohio Medical College in 1849, Gatling settled in Indianapolis, Indiana, where he would spend the next twenty years. During the 1850s, he spent most of his time speculating in real estate and railroad ventures, none of which did very well. In 1854, at the age of 36, he married Jemima T. Sanders, the daughter of an Indianapolis physician.

In the late 1850s, Gatling's attention again turned to invention. He patented five inventions in 1860, beginning a pattern that would be repeated throughout his life: when ideas struck him, they apparently did so in waves. His life is characterized by a series of multiple patent applications, no doubt inspired by bursts of creative genius.

With the exception of the screw propeller, all of Gatling's inventions up to this time had been related to farm machinery and were driven by the needs of the era. If one accepts the premise that necessity is the mother of invention, it is only logical that the events beginning on 15 April 1861 led to what is perhaps Dr. Gatling's most well-known invention, the Gatling gun. On that date, Abraham Lincoln declared the United States to be in a state of insurrection, and the Civil War began.

The Civil War and the Gatling Gun

At the beginning of the Civil War, the Union faced a curious dichotomy with respect to its weapons procurement policies. President Lincoln and other senior government officials openly encouraged the invention of new weapons to give the United States a

The Gatling
Gun: 19th
Century
Machine Gun
to 21st
Century
Vulcan

2

technological edge and a speedy victory. However, Col. (later Brig. Gen.) John W. Ripley, the army's chief of ordnance, strongly resisted any move away from standard-issue weapons.

Gatling invented his gun just a few months after the Civil War started. He had the prototype built in late 1861 or early 1862 and held firing demonstrations before prominent Indianapolis-area politicians and military officers. The reaction was generally favorable, but sales were slow.

One reason for this was the opposition of Colonel Ripley. Gatling circumvented this by demonstrating the Gatling gun to Maj. Gen. Benjamin Butler in 1863. Butler was so impressed that he immediately purchased twelve of the thirteen prototypes and used them in the Battle of Petersburg in June 1864, the first documented use of the Gatling gun in combat. All of this was handled informally, however. None of Butler's actions were sanctioned through the army's normal ordnance procurement channels (i.e., through Colonel Ripley).

Unlike the army, the navy agreed to a formal demonstration of the Gatling gun. Adm. John Dahlgren (chief of the Navy Bureau of Ordnance) personally observed the trials held in the Washington Navy Yard in May and July of 1863. Dahlgren was impressed and authorized fleet commanders to purchase Gatling guns if they so desired.

Gatling also tried to sell Gatling guns overseas during this time. Before a sale to France went through, however, the United States prohibited selling weapons to foreign nations for the remainder of the war.

Other reasons the Gatling gun saw limited acceptance and use during the Civil War included the military's lack of knowledge about machine guns, both from a mechanical and a tactical perspective, and the poor reliability and hazardous operation of other early machine guns. Also, Dr. Gatling's sympathies were rumored to be with the South. Some even believed that the first Gatling guns were manufactured in Cincinnati because of its close proximity to the Confederacy. No evidence was produced to substantiate the rumors, although their origins are understandable, considering Gatling's Southern roots. Still, Gatling never attempted to market his weapon to the South, even when he received a less-than-enthusiastic response from the Union army. The South traded materiel of war freely with European nations, and it would have been to Gatling's advantage to align himself with the Confederacy to further his plans for foreign sales. But since Gatling's first military sale was to Maj. Gen. Benjamin Butler, who was particularly despised by the South, the rumor's credibility seems questionable at best.

The question of Gatling's allegiance became moot on 9 April 1865, when Lee surrendered to Grant at Appomattox and the Civil War ended.

On 9 May 1865, Gatling patented an improved version of his original gun that used modern cartridges instead of individually loaded chambers. Maj. Gen. A.B. Dyer, who replaced Ripley as chief of army ordnance after the war, greeted the new Model 1865 with a more receptive attitude.

He ordered official trials of the Gatling gun in January 1865, and in August 1866, the U.S. Army officially approved use of the Gatling gun.

Overseas Marketing Successes

Acceptance by the U.S. Army was a major selling point in pursuing other contracts and proved to be a major factor in the success of the Gatling gun.

Gatling spent most of the remainder of the 1860s traveling throughout Europe, demonstrating the gun to military and other government officials. The first overseas military sale was to Russia in 1867. A sale to Turkey quickly followed, and the pattern of success continued. The Gatling gun became widely recognized as a superior weapon, and by the mid-1880s the armed forces of almost every nation in the world included Gatling guns among their inventories.

The Colt Connection

Gatling moved from Indianapolis to Hartford, Connecticut, in 1870, once his extensive overseas marketing effort had gained momentum. By that time, he had struck an exclusive deal with the Hartford-based Colt Company for the domestic production of Gatling guns, and he wanted to be close to the production base.

More Inventions

Over the next several years (through the mid- to late 1880s), Gatling spent most of his time marketing and developing new models of the Gatling gun. His penchant for invention was not restricted solely to the Gatling gun, however.

In the late 1870s, he focused on a torpedo gun designed to launch a 1.45-inch projectile from a 50-

Figure 1. Dr. Richard Jordan Gatling and one of his Gatling guns from the original Gatling Gun Company archives. (Photo courtesy of the Connecticut State Library and Museum.)

Compliments of R.J. Gatling

Hartford, May 1st 1893.

inch barrel (a very long barrel in those days). Unfortunately, the gun burst a barrel and injured a gunner during testing in late 1881, and the project ended shortly thereafter.

Undaunted by the failure, Gatling began work on a new weapon. In 1883, following up on his fascination with steam and compressed air, Gatling invented a single-barreled machine gun that could use either steam or compressed air to operate. Building on this concept, he also invented a loading system that could be operated by steam or compressed air. The new gun and its loading system were patented separately on 10 February 1885.

Gatling also developed a variety of new Gatling gun models offering improvements in mounts, sights, elevation and traversing systems, and barrel configurations. New models were developed for specialized applications, including police duty, naval use, and lightweight guns for light infantry units (see Chapter 3 for a complete discussion of the different Gatling gun models).

By the late 1880s, Gatling was more than seventy years old, but the pace of his inventions and patents suggests that his mind had not slowed at all. As had occurred at earlier times in Gatling's life, his creative genius again flourished with a machine-gun-like volley of new inventions.

The Electric Gatling Gun

In 1890, the U.S. Navy contracted with the Crocker-Wheeler Electric Motor Company of New York City to develop an electrically powered Gatling gun. Although the results were impressive, the navy expressed no further interest in the project.

Gatling, however, took a keen interest in it. His concept for an electric Gatling gun emerged three years later, on 25 July 1893, when he patented his version. Like the navy's Crocker-Wheeler electrically powered Gatling gun, Gatling's design was intended for use on ships. The reasons for this were simple: ships could supply electrical power; the army's infantry and artillery units could not.

One of the most significant differences between the navy's version and the one Gatling patented in 1893 was that Gatling's had a firing rate of 3,000 shots per minute, compared to 1,500 shots per minute for the navy's (interestingly, both rates are within the range of today's modern Gatling guns). Both rates of fire were incredibly high for the era, which probably contributed to the demise of the concept. In those days, there simply was no need for firing at such a high rate. In addition, supplying ammunition to such a system prevented severe logistical problems. For the next few years, Gatling, by now in his mid-seventies, turned to other projects.

In 1891, the American Association of Inventors and Manufacturers was founded in Washington, D.C., and Gatling served as its first president (an indication of the status he enjoyed in the industrial and technical communities of the era). In 1897, at the age of 79, he and his wife left Indianapolis and moved in with their daughter and son-in-law, Ida and Hugh Pentecost, in New York City.

The Final Years

In the later years of his life, Gatling focused on inventions and business ventures related primarily to agriculture, although there were exceptions. Around 1900, he began to suffer from a heart condition, although the problem had little effect on his creativity. He continued to patent a flurry of inventions until 1902, when he moved to St. Louis and organized the Gatling Motor Plow Company. It was only a few months, however, before he fell ill and returned to New York. On 26 February 1903, at the age of 84, Richard Jordan Gatling died. He was buried four days later in the family cemetery in Indianapolis.

2 The Gatling Principle of Operation

Richard Jordan Gatling stared at the Union black-powder rifle in front of him. It was slender and graceful, yet lethal. Although a skilled rifleman could use it to kill a man at 100 yards, Gatling knew that it was painfully slow to load, and once it had fired, its owner was completely exposed during the reloading process. Gatling had studied several weapons that could fire repeatedly, including the ill-fated "Coffee Grinder" and the French Mitrailleuse, but all had serious defects. The Coffee Grinder jammed frequently, and it had been known to blow up and kill its gunners. The Mitrailleuse was notoriously unreliable, and Union officers refused to even consider it. Early casualties in the war between the states were high, and Gatling knew that the Union forces needed new weaponry if the war was to be brought to a speedy close. Lincoln himself had encouraged the development of new armaments. Perhaps, Gatling reasoned, if a new weapon could fire rapidly enough, it would be so formidable that men would recognize the futility of war and abandon the idea of armed conflict entirely.

Fundamental Concepts

The original Gatling gun used a percussion firing system. All subsequent models (starting with the Model 1865) used metallic cartridges.

The Percussion Firing System

When most people think of loading a gun, they visualize it as a simple operation in which cartridges are inserted into the weapon (or a magazine). Most understand that the cartridges of modern weapons include both the bullet and the gunpowder. This simplicity of operation was not always the case. Earlier shooters had to use a much more complex percussion firing system. Unlike today's guns (most of which use metallic cartridges), shooters with percussion firing guns could not simply load a cartridge into their guns and fire. Instead, percussion shooters had to load the primer, gun powder, and bullet into their guns separately for each shot.

Figure 2 shows the basic elements of a percussion firing system, which consists of a gun barrel and a nipple (the nipple is an extension with a channel).

Figure 2. Percussion firing system operation.

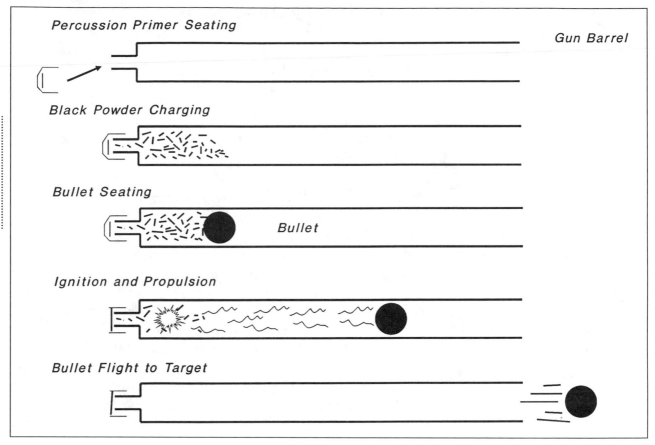

Loading began by placing a percussion primer on the nipple (as shown in the upper left portion of Figure 2). Black powder was then loaded into the barrel from the muzzle and tapped down prior to installing the bullet. The bullet (usually a round lead ball) was pressed into the barrel, again from the muzzle end (for this reason, percussion weapons are often referred to as "muzzleloaders"). Once the bullet was fully seated against the powder, the weapon was ready to fire.

A percussion weapon was fired by cocking the hammer and then releasing it to strike the percussion cap. The percussion cap contained a small quantity of an impact-sensitive material, which detonated when the hammer struck the cap. This detonation sent shock and heat waves through the channel in the nipple to the black powder. When the black powder ignited, it developed high pressure, which drove the bullet through the barrel with enough velocity upon exiting to continue its flight to the target. As the bullet moved down the barrel, it was engaged by spiral grooves machined into the barrel's inner surface (these grooves are called "rifling"), which imparted a spin to the bullet. The spin stabilized the bullet, making it more accurate. Once the bullet had left the bore, the spent percussion cap could be removed and the loading and firing process could begin again.

Army Weapon Preferences

During the Civil War, percussion weapon systems were standard-issue items (even though completely self-contained metallic cartridges had already been invented, the Union army had not yet adopted the concept).

A refinement of the percussion priming system that bridged the gap between percussion priming and metallic cartridges had been at least partially accepted by the Union army. It involved the use of integral paper-patched bullets and powder charges. Figure 3 shows the paper-patched bullet and powder concept. Paper-patched bullets and powder charges were loaded as a single unit into the muzzle of the gun (thereby eliminating the need to carry and load bullets and powder separately). When a gun loaded with these cartridges fired, the percussion primer gas jet perforated the paper bag attached to the bullet to ignite the powder. The gun then operated in the same manner described earlier.

Gatling recognized the futility of proposing a gun with metallic cartridges to the Union army and therefore opted to develop his first Gatling gun with paper-patched bullets and powder charges. He developed the first Gatling gun in 1862, accordingly designating it the Model 1862. It was to be the only variant of the Gatling gun that did not use the more modern metallic cartridges, and because of that, certain features of its operational sequence differ from later models. Nonetheless, its operation is worth studying, as it provides insight into the mechanical genius behind the weapon and a fundamental understanding of the operational concepts behind all future Gatling guns (including those used in many of today's modern weapon systems).

Gatling Gun Operation

As the above description demonstrates, the loading and firing of

Figure 3. Paper-patched bullets. The paper bullet patch engaged the rifling and also contained gunpowder to propel the bullet. When the gun fired, the primer burned through the paper to ignite the powder.

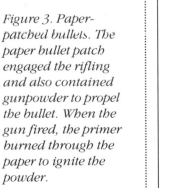

percussion weapons was a slow and cumbersome operation that left the gunner essentially defenseless during the reloading operation. This disadvantage was primarily responsible for the advent of metallic cartridges. The complexity of the reloading process was also a major design challenge in developing a high-rate-of-fire weapon, as were the cocking, hammer release, and recocking actions.

The elegance of the Gatling gun design is that the steps involved in loading and firing occur automatically. To understand how this occurs, one must first be familiar with another important mechanical concept, the principle of the cam.

A cam is simply a device that translates motion in one direction into motion in another direction (see Figure 4). It involves the motion of an inclined surface, which is then used to drive a follower. If the inclined surface is wrapped around a rotating surface, the rotating element can be used to create a back-and-forth (or reciprocating) motion in the follower. This is the concept Dr. Gatling used to drive the mechanism of the Gatling gun.

The problem Dr. Gatling solved was generating the reciprocating

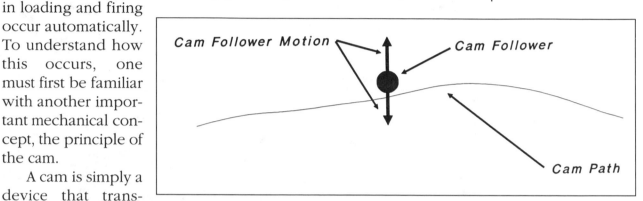

Figure 4. The concept of a cam. As the cam moves with respect to the cam follower, the cam follower will move in accordance with the profile of the cam.

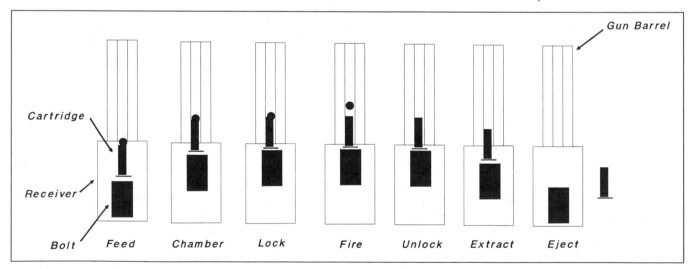

motion required to step through the actions of firing a gun. This cam-driven concept is shown in Figure 5, wherein the position of the gun mechanism is shown at successive stages of the firing process. In the first position, the gun drive mechanism is near the most narrow portion of the inclined cam surface.

Figure 5. Gatling firing sequence. As the gun mechanism rotates, the bolts are driven back and forth by the elliptical cam path.

Note that there are two ways a cam can be used to create reciprocating motion: the cam can be driven to actuate the followers, or the followers can be driven while the cam is held stationary. Dr. Gatling chose the latter approach, for reasons that will soon become obvious.

As the gun mechanism moves with respect to the cam, the hammer is pushed back, compressing a spring and cocking the gun. When the hammer is fully rearward (and its drive spring fully compressed), it encounters a sharp step on the cam profile. The cam step is a release, and it allows the drive spring to snap the hammer into the percussion cap. This fires the gun.

In our discussion above (and in Figure 5), we depicted a stationary cam surface, as well as a gun barrel and firing mechanism that moved with respect to the stationary cam. It involved a flat cam surface and a lateral motion of the gun along this surface. Let's take this one step further. Suppose the entire gun mechanism (moving gun barrel and action and cam) is wrapped around a shaft parallel to the gun barrel (as shown in Figure 6). The barrel, hammer, and other elements of the gun's action would then revolve around this central axis. Suppose further that the cam is wrapped around the interior of a stationary cylindrical housing at the rear of the gun. We'd then have a design in which the gun barrel and action spun around, and the action was driven through the firing steps by the stationary cylindrical cam inside the rear housing. While completing its journey around the inside of the housing, the cam would cock and release the hammer, just as was described earlier.

Figure 6. Gatling cam-path-driven operation. As the gun mechanism rotates, the cam follower moves the bolt back and forth, accomplishing the Gatling gun firing sequence.

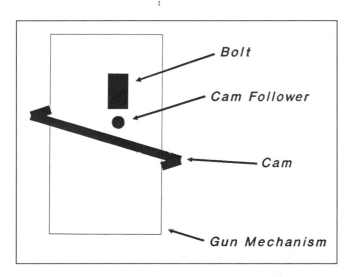

Bolt

Cam Follower

Cam

Gun Mechanism

Once the gun operation and rotary gun mechanism/stationary cam concepts are understood, the remaining theory of the operation of the Gatling gun is straightforward. All that's involved are the additional actions required to load the gun prior to firing and eject the spent cartridge after firing.

The design need not be restricted to only one gun action and barrel. Other actions and barrels can also mount on the central axis, and these can make the circular journey around the stationary cam simultaneously. The number of additional actions and barrels is constrained only by size (how many will fit around the axis and the stationary cam) and weight (if the gun design is limited to a specified weight). The first Gatling gun (the Model 1862) had six barrels, but it could just as easily have had more or fewer.

To simplify our discussion, let's follow the path of one barrel and action around the circular cam. The Model 1862 operated with five basic steps:

- loading
- compression
- locking and firing
- unlocking
- ejecting

Each step occurred as the Gatling gun mechanism revolved inside the stationary, circular cam path. The mechanism was driven by the familiar small hand crank at the rear of the weapon. When the crank was turned, a small pinion gear on the end of it engaged a larger ring gear on the cluster of gun barrels and actions. This large ring gear was fixed to the main shaft of the gun. When the main shaft rotated, the entire barrel assembly and all of the other moving parts (each barrel's actions, etc.) rotated counterclockwise (as viewed from the muzzle end). As these components moved, followers in each barrel's action followed the circular cam path in the stationary rear housing.

Loading

At the beginning of this chapter, we described how a basic percussion-fired weapon operates and then progressed into an explanation of paper cartridges. As you will recall, the first steps required placing a percussion cap on the nipple and a paper cartridge and bullet in the barrel.

Gatling recognized that these actions could not be easily accomplished while the gun mechanism he envisioned was spinning around a circular cam path. It would be difficult to ram paper cartridges into a spinning barrel and delicately place the percussion caps on moving seats. Gatling solved the problem by preloading steel chambers with paper cartridges, bullets, and percussion caps, and then loading these into the Gatling gun feed mechanism.

These preloaded steel chambers have been described as miniature guns. In a sense they were, but they could perhaps be more accurately described as predecessors to the metallic cartridge. They were self-contained units with a projectile, propellant, and primer, invented solely to simplify loading. Metallic cartridges were smaller and easier to load, but the concept was nearly identical.

The Model 1862 Gatling gun had a small hopper on top of the gun mechanism (near the rear). A quantity of the preloaded steel chambers was placed into the hopper, and as the gun mechanism turned, the chambers fell into grooves in the gun's rotating mechanism. The gun had a grooved slot for each barrel. When each groove passed approximately through the two o'clock position, one of the preloaded chambers from the hopper dropped into place. The groove aligned the preloaded chamber with the bore of the gun barrel so that when the chamber fired, the bullet had a straight shot into the barrel. As the gun mechanism turned, each preloaded chamber traveled with its barrel, remaining in constant alignment with it.

Compression

As the gun mechanism continued to rotate, a protrusion on the hammer engaged the cam surface. At this point, the lock cylinder actuated. The lock cylinder consisted of a tube containing a hammer and a compression spring. A protrusion on the hammer extended through a groove in the lock cylinder tube to contact the circular cam path. As the gun mechanism continued to rotate, the hammer spring approached full compression (near the twelve o'clock position).

Locking and Firing

Just prior to reaching the twelve o'clock position, the rear of the lock cylinder contacted a small raised surface in the rear of the housing, formed by a hardened steel insert in the plate behind the gun mechanism. The insert was designed to force the lock cylinder forward, which in turn forced the preloaded chamber against the rear of its gun barrel. This caused the forward surface of the preloaded chamber to bear down against the barrel, "locking" it into position and forming a better seal. The concept was to effect a better seal, thereby minimizing the escape of propellant gases and providing for higher bullet velocity.

As soon as locking occurred, the hammer protrusion (in the locking cylinder) reached a sharp forward step on the cam surface, which released the hammer. The hammer spring drove it into the percussion cap, firing the preloaded chamber.

Unlocking

Once the barrel had fired, it had to be unloaded so it could be reloaded and fired again. Before this could be done, though, the locking action had to be unlocked. This was governed by the proper sizing and positioning of the small insert described above. Once the lock cylinder passed the insert (as the gun mechanism continued to turn) another spring on the outside of the cylinder pushed it slightly to the rear. This relieved some of the pressure holding the preloaded (and now fired) chamber against the barrel. The remaining force holding the chamber against the gun barrel came from the hammer spring, which now (in the fired position) held the hammer against the percussion cap and the chamber against the barrel. Dr. Gatling included another small raised surface on the cam path to back the hammer away from the steel chamber just enough to allow the chamber to float freely. This occurred as the gun progressed from the eleven o'clock position to the ten o'clock position.

Ejection

The chamber could be ejected once it had unlocked. This occurred as the rotating cluster of barrels and actions positioned the now-fired chamber near the bottom of the gun. The chamber simply fell free through an opening in the base of the mechanism, where it could be picked up for later cleaning and reloading. To prevent the chambers from getting hung up in the gun mechanism, a guide bar forced them out as the chamber groove passed through the six o'clock position.

Once the five steps described above were complete, the now-empty chamber groove (in the rotating cluster) continued its circular journey up to the hopper, where a new preloaded chamber fell into position and the load, compress, lock, fire, unlock, and eject process began again. As mentioned earlier, the Model 1862 Gatling gun had six sets of barrels, actions, and grooves. These spun as a set, with each of the steps described above occurring sequentially. The gun fired six times with each rotation of the barrel cluster.

The Model 1862 was the only Gatling gun to use the separate preloaded chambers. There were several problems inherent to this approach, which were corrected in subsequent versions of the gun. These problems and others (as well as the solutions and subsequent Gatling guns) are discussed in the next chapter. The use of metallic cartridges in the Model 1865 significantly changed the manner in which the Gatling gun operated. Though many of the detailed mechanical actions changed, all were actuated through the rotating-barrel-cluster and stationary-circular-cam approach. As will be seen in subsequent discussions on contemporary Gatling guns (starting with Chapter 6), all modern variants of the Gatling use this approach.

CHAPTER 3 The Early Gatling Guns

*T**he old ordnance sergeant rested his hand on the Gatling's rear housing assembly as he pondered the history of the magnificent weapon. From the Civil War through the Indian Wars and on into countless other conflicts, the Gatling gun had done its job well. The sergeant's thoughts drifted back nearly forty years to when he was a raw recruit on the plains of New Mexico and a .45/70 Gatling saved him from an Apache patrol. What the Gatling had inflicted upon the Apaches was gut-wrenching, but certainly no more so than what the Apaches would have done to him had they prevailed. The sergeant ran his old hand across the newer but soon-to-be-obsolete .30-caliber Gatling gun. The metal was cold, but it felt hauntingly warm, and somehow reassuring. The history of the weapon and the action it had seen paralleled the development of the United States from the Civil War through the settling of the West and into a new century. We're both retiring now, he thought. We're both relics of an era past.*

There are two categories of Gatling guns: those of the pre-Vulcan era (from the first Model 1862 to the Model 1903, which were generally used from the Civil War through the Spanish-American War), and those of the modern era (starting with the post World War II search for a modern high-rate-of-fire cannon). This chapter addresses the early Gatling guns, a summary of which is presented in the table on page 16.

Gatling Gun Models and Specifications

In all, Dr. Gatling developed more than thirty variants of the Gatling gun during a period exceeding forty years. The early Gatlings were chambered in more than a dozen calibers for U.S. forces alone, reflecting the changing weapons preferences of the times. The first Gatling gun (described in Chapter 2) fired percussion-primed paper cartridges. Later models included cartridge variants up to 1 inch in caliber. Muzzle velocities reflected the variations in chambering, ranging from less than 1,000 feet per second (fps) to more than 3,000 fps.

When the specifications for the early Gatling guns are examined either individually or as a group, the inventive genius of Dr. Gatling becomes evident. The evolution of the early Gatling guns was perhaps second to none of that era and is mirrored in the continuing improvement of today's Gatling guns.

Dr. Gatling's ability to adapt his invention to continually evolving

Table 3-1. Gatling gun models and specifications.

Table 3-1
Gatling Gun Models and Specifications

Model	Variants	Caliber(s)	User(s)	Features
1862	None	.58	U.S Army	Preloaded steel chambers.
1865	1866	.58, .50, and 1-inch	U.S. Army	Metallic cartridges, redesigned operating mechanism, 6- and 10-barrel variants, first official U.S. Army procurement.
1871	None	.42, .50, .65, and 1-inch	U.S. Army, Russian Army	Improved bolt and feed system design (Broadwell drum); 5-, 6-, and 10-barrel variants; automatic oscillatory (traverse) feature.
1874	Bulldog Gatling, Camel Gun, 1875, 1876, 1877	.43, .45, .50, .55, .65, .75, and 1-inch	U.S. Army and several foreign users	Short- and long-barreled (18-inch and 32-inch) versions, reduced size and weight, improved headspacing features, improved ocsillator, simplified feed system, tripod mounting.
1879	None	.45	U.S. Army and several foreign users	Fully enclosed barrels, simplified elevation and traverse mechanism, further headspacing improvements, ten 32-inch barrels.
1881	None	.45	U.S. Army and several foreign users	Bruce feed mechanism, exposed barrels.
1883	1885, 1886, 1887	.45	U.S. Army, U.S. Navy, and several foreign users	Accles feed, selective crank placement, 1500-rpm firing rate, strengthened internal mechanism, cocking switch, elevation and traverse improvements, fully enclosed barrels.
1889	Police Gatling, 1891, 1892	.45	U.S. Army, police agencies	Exposed barrels, feed system improvements, all-metal carriage.
1893	None	.30/40	U.S. Army, U.S. Navy	Strengthened internal components to handle higher chamber pressures, strip feed system, modified headspace adjustment, armored protection.
1895	None	.30/40	U.S. Army, U.S. Navy	Improved metallurgy, Bruce feed system, painted/blued components, improved armor protection, multiple barrel configurations.
1900	Navy version	.30/40	U.S. Army, U.S. Navy	Interchangeable bolts, optional crank location, special Navy variant with full bronze barrel enclosure.
1903	1903-06	.30-03, .30-06	U.S. Army	Incorporated new Springfield .30-caliber cartridge, last operational Gatling gun of the early era.

military needs kept the Gatling gun a viable weapon for five decades. Few weapons of any period can make such a claim. This chapter addresses each of the nine major early Gatling gun models, as well as variants of each. The major Gatling gun categories are designated by numbers that denote the first year of introduction.

Model 1862

The Model 1862 was the first version of the Gatling gun. This model was significantly different from all those that followed. The Model 1862 was the only Gatling gun to use preloaded chambers and percussion-primed paper cartridges. Many of the engineering challenges Dr. Gatling faced in designing this model were unique to the preloaded chambers, while others affected all models. The problems created by the Model 1862's preloaded chamber feed system were serious, and with the U.S. Army's gradual move to metallic cartridge ammunition, the direction of future Gatling guns was clear.

The Model 1862's preloaded chambers had a serious problem with gas leakage at the chamber-to-barrel interface. The gas leakage reduced both muzzle velocity (some of the propellant gases escaped prior to the bullet exiting) and reliability (the escaping gases fouled the gun's action and drive mechanism). As mentioned in Chapter 2, Gatling addressed this issue with a design feature that forced the chamber against the barrel just prior to firing (the very first Model 1862 did not have this feature, but Gatling added it to later Model 1862s when the severity of the gas leakage became apparent).

This was only partially effective at sealing the chamber to the barrel. Dr. Gatling soon recognized that the forcing feature created another problem. Because the separate steel insert wedged the preloaded chambers against the barrel, it made the guns harder to crank.

A third variant of the Model 1862 actually incorporated metallic cartridges (a .58-caliber rimfire cartridge), but it retained the separate preloaded chambers. (Metallic cartridges were invented about seventeen years prior to the Gatling gun, but again, they had not yet been adopted by the U.S. military.) Dr. Gatling no doubt kept the separate preloaded chambers because he recognized the inherent advantages of metallic cartridges and wanted to quickly field a metallic cartridge version of the gun without the delays a major redesign would entail.

Another problem with the preloaded chambers was that it was difficult to keep machining tolerances tight enough to maintain precise alignment between the preloaded chamber and the barrel. Dr. Gatling's Model 1862 patent extolled the alignment virtues of each chamber traveling with its own barrel, but in practice, the desired alignment proved to be elusive. Minor misalignments (perhaps on the order of only a few thousandths of an inch) would result in the barrel "shaving" the bullet as it traveled from the chamber to the barrel. The result was inaccuracy (induced by bullet distortion) and rapid fouling of the gun's action and drive mechanism. In an attempt to solve this problem, Gatling used barrels with tapered bores, with a slightly larger diameter at the breech end. The hope was that the barrel would act as a funnel, allowing some misalignment that would be overcome as the barrel gradually guided the bullet through its bore. Although this concept was similar to the forcing cones used in early and contemporary revolvers, it was not effective in the Model 1862. The bullets were damaged more by bouncing around in the tapered bore than they were when fired into a nontapered barrel, and poor accuracy resulted.

The preloaded chambers were also a logistics concern. The army had no provisions for separate chambers. The time required to clean and load them greatly detracted from the Model 1862's combat readiness. One option was to preload a large number of chambers, but that created weight and other transportation problems. Simply stated, the logistics of a weapon requiring a totally unique ammunition and loading approach was more of a burden than the army cared to take on.

Gatling recognized the problems created by the preloaded chambers and realized that his invention would probably never succeed either commercially or tactically unless these deficiencies were met head on. He knew the answer to these problems could be found in metallic cartridges. Although the U.S. military had not yet officially adopted them, their advantages were so overwhelming and apparent that Gatling knew the conversion was only a matter of time. Near the end of the Civil War, he began work on a version of the Gatling gun that used metallic cartridges and did away with the preloaded chamber concept.

Model 1865

The Model 1865 Gatling gun significantly improved upon the original Model 1862 design. While it was not the first Gatling to use metallic cartridges, it was the first to eliminate the separate preloaded chambers. In the Model 1865, the chambers were an integral part of each barrel, as is the case with most modern weapons (including modern versions of the Gatling gun).

Integral chambers eliminated the gas sealing, excessive friction, misalignment, tapered bore, accuracy, and logistics problems, but these problems were replaced by others. Dr. Gatling now faced the challenge of developing a reliable means of feeding, inserting, chambering, and extracting each cartridge instead of simply dropping a preloaded chamber from a hopper into a groove in the gun's inner mechanism. (The problem was not an insignificant one. The feed mechanism and associated technology for today's Gatling guns often push the limits of mechanical engineering. There are two defense contractors who work only in this area.)

Dr. Gatling retained the basic Model 1862 theory of operation (a circular cam path to reciprocate each barrel's action) and added features to perform the chambering and extraction functions.

Separate bolt mechanisms were incorporated for each barrel. The bolts rode on rails that revolved with the barrels, and as the entire mechanism turned, the bolts were made to reciprocate in the same manner as the Model 1862's hammers did in their lock cylinders. The reciprocating motion took the bolts through the chamber, lock, fire, unlock, and eject sequence.

The Model 1865 was fired by a spring-loaded firing pin. The firing pin was driven rearward to compress its drive spring and was subsequently released through the action of a separate cam path.

The Model 1865 was the first Gatling gun in which the army took a serious (and official) interest. The first Model 1865 Dr. Gatling provided for the army trials had four barrels and was chambered for the .58-caliber rimfire round. This differed from the Model 1862, which had six barrels. Barrel variations (both length and number) were common during the early history of the Gatling gun, just as they are today. Such variations could be used to change the weight, firing rate, and cost of the gun. The exact reason that the first Model 1865 had four barrels instead of six is unknown. The army's tests of this version were successful, but the four-barrel configuration was dropped at the conclusion of the trial's initial phase, and the army asked Dr. Gatling to build a 1-inch caliber version for further tests.

Gatling designed this variant with six barrels, providing the army with eight guns. These were also very successful.

Gatling received his first official U.S. government contract in 1866. The army ordered one hundred Gatling guns—fifty ten-barreled .50-caliber guns and fifty six-barreled 1-inch-caliber guns. The .50-caliber guns fired the .50/70/450 designation, which was standard U.S. infantry issue. (The .50/70/450 designation meant that the cartridge had a .50-inch diameter projectile propelled by 70 grains of black powder, and that the projectile weighed 450 grains.) Because the contract was awarded in 1866, the army designated these Gatling guns Model 1866, although they were essentially identical to the Model 1865s.

One of the problems discovered after the first guns were delivered to the army was a timing anomaly. Each barrel was supposed to fire at approximately the ten o'clock position (when viewed from the front of the gun). The spring that snapped the firing pin into the primer required a small period of time to drive the firing pin fully forward, and if the gun was operated fast enough, the firing barrel could pass its intended firing position before the bullet left the muzzle. The result was that the bullet would occasionally impact the front of the gun frame.

Dr. Gatling's fix was simple. Later Model 1866 Gatling guns (and all subsequent models with exposed barrels and frames) had inverted U-shaped notches in the front of the frame, the sole purpose of which was to provide added clearance between the frame and the exiting bullet.

The timing problem was corrected, but other problems soon surfaced. The result was a significant redesign, which became the Model 1871.

Model 1871

Among the problems and shortcomings inherent to the Model 1865 was the fact that it could not be traversed unless the entire gun carriage was moved (this was tactically disadvantageous, as it made it essentially impossible to laterally sweep an area with gunfire while the weapon was firing).

In addition, the bolts frequently failed. They were extremely difficult to remove, which no doubt interfered with routine cleaning of the gun and probably contributed to the failures.

The feed system was also marginal (although one must take into consideration that there was no precedent for high-rate-of-fire feed systems in 1865). This caused frequent jams. (As mentioned earlier, feed system technology was a completely new area when the Gatling gun was developed, and even today, modern Gatling gun feed systems are impressively complex. Gatling continued to develop feed system improvements throughout his life, and work in this area continues to this day for contemporary Gatlings.)

The Model 1871 corrected most of these deficiencies. A feature that allowed the gunner to laterally traverse the gun without moving the carriage was a major improvement. Dr. Gatling also included a feature that induced an automatic oscillatory lateral motion as the gun fired. He simply extended the gun crank through the gun and inserted the opposite end into a fixed cam track. When the gunner turned the crank to fire the gun, the gun was also forced to oscillate slightly from side to side. This greatly increased the Gatling gun's lethality, allowing it to effectively spray an area with gunfire.

Gatling redesigned the breech bolts to eliminate the failures and added an access port at the rear of the gun to facilitate removal of the bolts for cleaning. This was a significant maintenance improvement for the gunners. Earlier Gatlings required disassembling most of the gun to gain access to the bolts.

Two improved feed systems were developed for the Model 1871. The first incorporated a curved magazine rather than the simple hopper used in the Model 1862 and Model 1865. The curved magazine contained a single column of vertically stacked cartridges. Except for the fact that it was mounted on top of the gun, the Model 1871's magazine was quite similar to the large-capacity "banana" magazines used on modern assault weapons.

Not quite satisfied with the capacity of the curved magazine, Dr.

Gatling asked L.M. Broadwell (his overseas sales agent) to develop a larger-capacity feed system. The Broadwell drum was a set of twenty vertical magazines that were mated in a circular manner (thus forming a drum). Each contained twenty cartridges. The fully loaded drum contained 400 hundred rounds. The drum mounted on top of the gun. As each magazine was depleted, the gunner manually positioned the drum to align the next set of twenty cartridges.

Model 1871 Gatling guns were chambered in several calibers (.42, .50, .65, and 1 inch). They were manufactured in five-, six-, and ten-barrel versions. The army recognized that the Model 1871 was a significantly improved weapon. As a result, it conducted a new series of Gatling gun trials in late 1873 to evaluate the improved versions. The army tested the guns in .42- and 1-inch caliber. The .42-caliber gun was a Russian export model with design improvements specified by Colonel Gorloff, a Russian ordnance officer. (As an aside, the Russians later claimed to have invented the Gatling gun, referring to it as a "Gorloff.") The army was particularly impressed with the performance of the smaller gun, which would become the Model 1874.

Figure 7. The Model 1874 Gatling gun. This version, which is on display at the Connecticut State Library and Museum, features tripod mounting and 32-inch barrels. It is chambered for the .45/70 cartridge, the standard infantry round of the era. The Model 1874 Gatling was also offered in other configurations, including the Bulldog and Camel.

Model 1874

After the 1873 trials, the army procured several guns of the new design in .45/70 caliber (this round had a .45-caliber bullet propelled by 70 grains of black powder). Two versions were produced: a short Gatling with 18-inch barrels and a long one with 32-inch barrels.

The Model 1874 offered several improvements over earlier versions, the first being reduced size and weight. The bolts were smaller than those used on previous Gatlings, which allowed the entire gun to be downsized accordingly.

Other features allowed improved headspacing and headspacing adjustment. (Headspace is the distance between the rear of the cartridge and the front of the bolt face when the cartridge is fully seated in the chamber. If the gun has excessive headspace, a large portion of the cartridge case will be unsupported, which could allow it to rupture.) The Gatling was the first high-rate-of-fire gun procured in significant quantities by the U.S. military, which did not yet have a full appreciation of the effects of high firing rates in terms of gun heating, gun wear, and so on. One of the findings was that as the Gatling gun fired, the heat it generated caused the gun's steel mainshaft to grow in length. When this occurred, headspace increased. Dr. Gatling's first attempt to address this phenomenon was on the Model 1874. He simply wrapped the mainshaft in leather to insulate it from heat.

On earlier models of the Gatling, headspace adjustment was accomplished by turning an adjusting nut located on the gun's frame in front of the barrel. This was an extremely hazardous operation. If the gun was still loaded (or even if it simply had ammunition in the feed system), applying torque to the headspace adjusting nut could turn the entire barrel cluster. This would have the same effect as turning the crank at the rear of the gun (i.e., the gun would fire). Several people were killed or injured performing this operation. To address this concern, Dr. Gatling incorporated a safety feature on the Model 1874 that locked the gun mechanism, rendering it incapable of firing.

The Model 1874 also featured an improved automatic oscillator. It was somewhat similar to the one used on the Model 1871 (it used a tracked cam on the end of the gun crankshaft that engaged a post attached to the gun carriage), but the Model 1874's design was much more straightforward, and it could also be used as a windage adjustment. On the 1874, the tracked cam had two paths. One was elliptical, which created a lateral oscillatory motion as the gun fired. The other was circular and was used to make the windage adjustment.

The Model 1874 also incorporated additional feed system improvements, including a provision for a simplified 40-round magazine on top of the gun. As a result of the magazine's location, the sights were relocated to the right side of the Model 1874. Some of the Model 1874 Gatlings were also equipped with Broadwell drums.

The lighter weight of the shorter Model 1874 (the 18-inch-barreled version) allowed for interesting mounting arrangements. Tripods were used for the first time. Special saddles for overseas customers were built to mount the Model 1874 on camels. Gatling made extensive use of this idea in his advertising, and as a result, the shorter Model 1874 became known as the Camel gun.

Models 1875-1877

Subsequent improvements resulted in the Model 1875, 1876, and 1877 Gatling guns. The Model 1875 had sturdier sights and bolt improvements to reduce jamming. The Model 1876 had stronger internal gun mechanism components, further modifications to the headspace adjustment, and improvements to the feed system. The Model 1877 incorporated more feed system improvements, as well as gearing changes to increase the firing rate. Models 1874 through 1877 were chambered in eight different calibers for U.S. and foreign customers, including .42, .43, .45, .50, .55, .65, .75, and 1-inch cartridges. Most of these were for foreign customers (the standard U.S. chambering was the .45/70 cartridge).

The Bulldog Gatling

The Bulldog Gatling, introduced in 1877, was the first Gatling to offer full enclosure of the barrels as a standard design feature, although a few fully enclosed Gatling guns had been manufactured previously for the navy (the navy preferred full barrel enclosure to protect the gun from the ocean's highly corrosive salt spray). The U.S. government purchased .45/70-caliber Bulldogs; other barrel and caliber variations were produced for export.

The Bulldog had several additional features that distinguished it from earlier models. One of note was the rear crankshaft, which incorporated three improvements. The first was a higher rate of fire. The crank was attached directly to the mainshaft of the gun (there was no gear reduction), allowing the Bulldog to fire at rates as high as 1,000 RPM. (Interestingly, this rate, achieved more than 100 years ago, is at the lower end of the range used by modern electrically or hydraulically powered Gatling guns.) Second, the Bulldog was the first Gatling gun to move the headspace adjustment to the rear of the gun, making for much safe opera-tion. Finally, the Bulldog's rear crank allowed a redesign of the traverse oscillator. Cranking the Bulldog automatically induced side-to-side forces on the gun. Dr. Gatling took advantage of this by placing a spring on either side of the gun, which allowed the lateral traverse limits to be adjusted by changing spring tension.

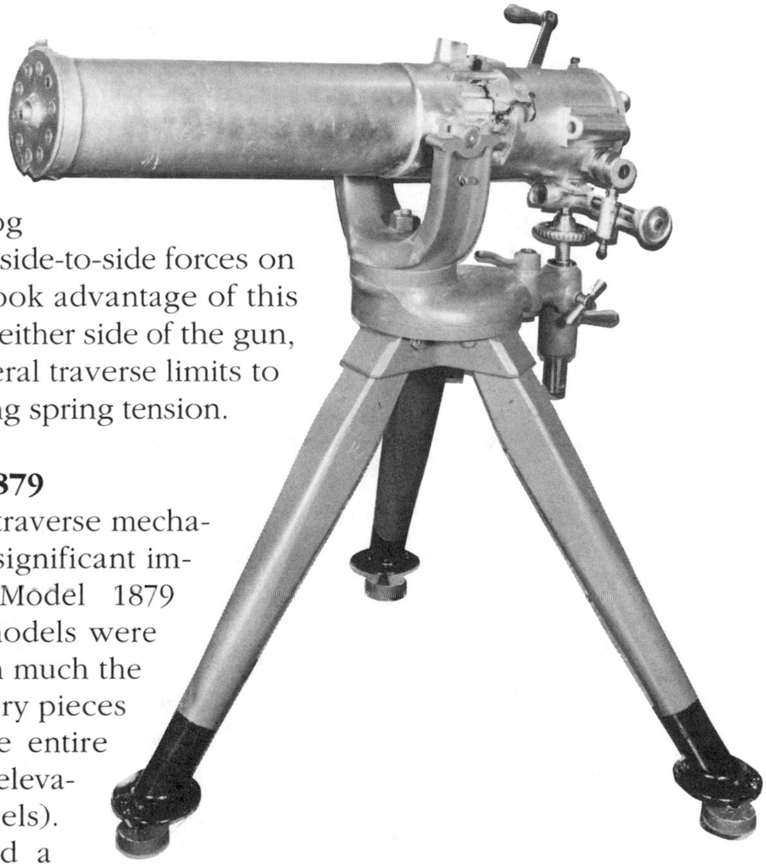

Figure 8. The Model 1879 Gatling gun. Note the ten fully enclosed barrels and the tripod mounting. The automatic oscillatory mechanism can also be seen at the rear of the weapon. The tubelike attachment at the rear of the receiver accepted a rod that allowed the gunner to quickly point the weapon at a target. Although the Model 1879 dropped the elevation and traverse adjusting wheels, this particular specimen retains these features (Gatlings were ordered with special features occasionally).

Model 1879

The elevation and traverse mechanisms were the most significant improvements to the Model 1879 Gatling gun. Earlier models were pointed at the target in much the same manner as artillery pieces (either by moving the entire carriage or by turning elevation and traverse wheels). The Model 1879 used a

The Gatling
Gun: 19th
Century
Machine Gun
to 21st
Century
Vulcan

24

Figure 9. An exploded photograph of the Model 1879 Gatling gun. Two of the gun's ten bolts are shown installed on the rails. The serrated knob at the rear of the weapon was incorporated to facilitate headspace adjustment.

much quicker method. It allowed the gunner to point the weapon with a simple rod attached to the rear of the gun. Once the gun was pointed at the target, both elevation and traverse could be locked in place.

Also, another minor improvement was incorporated into the headspace adjustment feature. Instead of requiring tools, this adjustment could now be accomplished by hand-turning a serrated knob mounted on the rear of the gun.

The Model 1879 had ten 32-inch barrels, which were chambered for the .45/70 cartridge and fully enclosed. By this time, Gatling had determined that the gun's users did not require the automatic traverse oscillator he had perfected, and it was thus dropped from the Model 1879 and all subsequent versions of the Gatling gun.

Model 1881

The Model 1881 Gatling gun differed from the Model 1879 in two ways. One was that it did not have a fully enclosed barrel cluster. The Model 1881 was developed for the U.S. Army, and the probable explanation for the return to exposed barrels is that the army was more concerned with lighter weight and mobility than protection from a salt-spray environment.

The most significant difference was incorporation of the Bruce feed mechanism. Patented by Lucien Bruce in 1881, this feed mechanism became recognized as the best Gatling gun ammunition handling system. The device was simple and reliable. It consisted of two rails that held ammunition. The rails were mounted on a pivot, which held one rail in alignment with the gun's feed port. Once the first rail was emptied, the weight of the cartridges in the other forced the dual-railed mechanism to seesaw into position such that the new rail's cartridges were aligned with the feed port. Firing could continue uninterrupted.

The Bruce rail offered another less obvious advantage. It allowed cartridges to be loaded directly from the ammunition box, being "poured" into the rail. Not having to load each cartridge into the magazine individually greatly speeded the loading operation and allowed for nearly continuous firing.

Model 1883

Two of the improvements made to the Model 1883 were carried through to modern military Gatlings, although one, the Accles feed, was unsuccessful.

The Accles feed was invented by James Accles, who represented the Gatling Gun Company in Europe and later went on to start his own machine gun business. The Accles feed was a large circular drum that mounted on top of the Gatling gun. A slotted wheel, driven by the gun's internal mechanism, turned within the drum as the gun fired. Cartridges were carried within slots machined in the wheel, and as the wheel turned, the cartridges followed a spiral track on the inside surface of the drum. The track drove the cartridges to the gun's feed port, where they entered the gun and then were cycled through the Gatling's firing sequence.

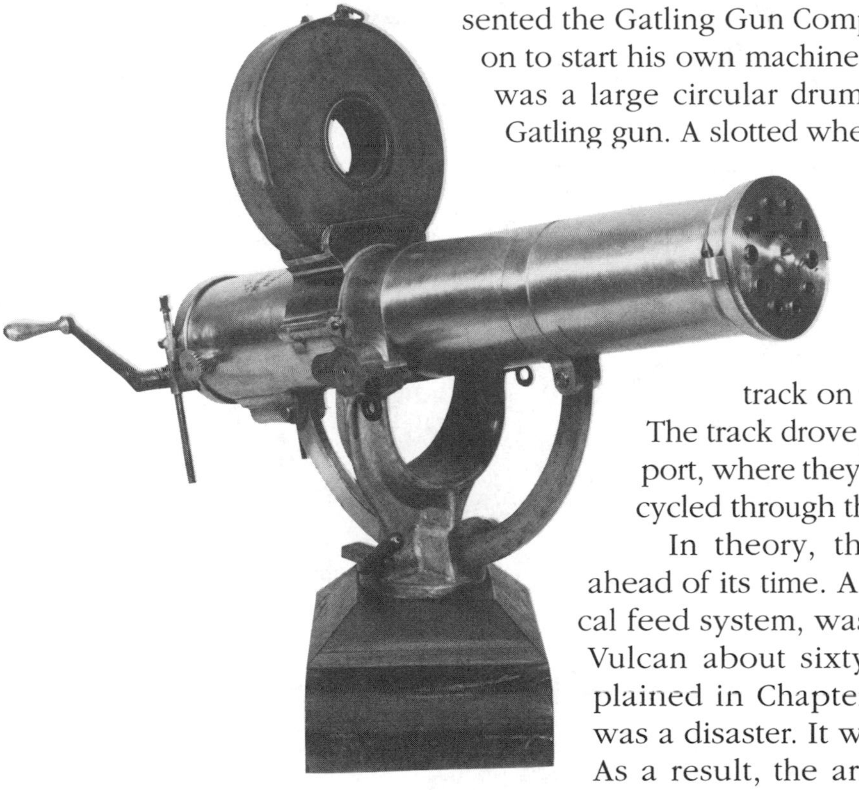

In theory, the Accles feed was decades ahead of its time. A similar arrangement, the helical feed system, was incorporated in the modern Vulcan about sixty years later (as will be explained in Chapter 8). In practice, however, it was a disaster. It was fragile and jammed easily. As a result, the army paid for a retrofit of the Accles feed system on all Model 1883 Gatling guns, replacing it with the Bruce feed described earlier.

Figure 10. The Model 1883 Gatling gun. This is a ten-barreled .45/70-caliber gun. Note the Accles feed drum mounted on top of the system and the sights on the right side of the weapon.

One of the successful features incorporated into the Model 1883 was selective crank placement. The gun could be operated with the crank on the side (as was common practice on earlier Gatlings) or attached directly to the rear of the gun's mainshaft. The side mount allowed a firing rate of 800 RPM; the rear mount was truly impressive, with a firing rate of 1,500 RPM. The rear mount's higher firing rate was a result of direct drive. The side-mounted crank fired more slowly because it operated through a reduction gear. To allow the gun to survive the higher firing rate, Dr. Gatling strengthened the bolts, extractors, and other parts of its internal mechanism.

The cocking switch was the viable feature of the Model 1883 that carried through to modern Gatlings. The cocking switch allowed the gunner to select two different cam paths for the firing pins. One path fired the gun normally; the other allowed the gun to be operated without cycling the firing pins. The second path was a useful training feature. It also allowed the gunner to clear the weapon without firing any rounds in the mechanism.

Minor improvements to the elevation and traverse mechanisms were also incorporated on Model 1883. These were primarily adaptations of features included on earlier Gatlings.

The Models 1885, 1886, and 1887 were all derivatives of the Model 1883, incorporating minor ejection mechanism improvements and other subtle design upgrades. The Model 1883 and all of its derivatives had ten barrels with the fully enclosed bronze jacket and were chambered for the .45/70 cartridge.

Model 1889

The Model 1889 was primarily an upgrade to the Model 1883 series. Aside from the Accles feed system, another detractor from the Model 1883 series Gatlings was the bronze jacket, which was difficult to manufacture. Dr. Gatling developed the Model 1889 to address these and other shortcomings.

The Model 1889 returned to the exposed-barrel configuration. Other upgrades included the Bruce feed system, an improved cocking switch, a nearly all-metal carriage (earlier versions were wood and metal), and armored shields to protect the gunner from enemy fire.

The Model 1889 was built from 1889 through 1892. Gatling guns procured in 1891 and 1892 were designated as Model 1891 and Model 1892 Gatlings, but they were essentially identical to the Model 1889. These guns all had ten 32-inch barrels chambered for the .45/70 cartridge.

The Gatling Police Model

Little is known about the Gatling Police Model (the Gatling Gun Company archives do not even include any reference to this model). The Police Gatlings are believed to have been manufactured in small quantities from the late 1880s to the early 1890s. Judging by a photo of Dr. Gatling with one of these models (found in the company archives), the Police Model was similar to the Model 1877 Bulldog, except that it had an Accles feed system and the Model 1883's elevation and traverse mechanism.

Model 1893

The U.S. Army adopted the .30/40 Krag as its standard infantry cartridge in 1892. Although weapons chambered for the older .45/70 cartridge remained in the inventory for a long time (the army was armed with obsolete .45/70 rifles in the War of 1898), a modern weapon was clearly desirable. The .30/40 Krag shot faster and flatter than the .45/70, and it delivered more energy to distant targets. Thus, it was only natural that the army would procure a new Gatling gun chambered for the .30/40 cartridge.

The Model 1893 was similar to the Model 1889, with slight improvements and upgrades to allow for firing the .30/40 Krag cartridge. The .30/40 operated with higher chamber pressures than the .45/70, so the internal gun mechanism of the Model 1893 was strengthened accordingly. The outer housing cam path was also altered to provide quicker actuation of the bolts.

The Model 1893 had a new strip-feed system that ultimately proved unsuccessful. The cartridges were loaded into strips that were then fed into the gun. As the Model 1893 fired, the cartridges were supposed to strip free of their carriers and feed into the gun. Unfortunately, the system jammed frequently. The problem was severe enough to require retrofitting all Model 1893 Gatling guns to the older and more reliable Bruce feed system.

Figure 11. The business end of a Model 1893 Gatling gun. Note the ten .30-caliber barrels and the crosshair sight mounted to the left of the muzzle.

The Model 1893 was chambered for the .30/40 Krag round, following the army's normal practice of using its issue infantry cartridge. During the Bruce feed system retrofit (which occurred in 1897), Gatling also modified the Model 1893's headspace adjustment mechanism to limit the adjustment range. Prior to this, the adjustment mechanism was essentially the same as that of the Model 1889. Gatling probably incorporated the limitation as a result of the .30/40's higher chamber pressure, as sensitivity to headspace adjustment increases with chamber pressure. Since improperly adjusted headspace could result in severe gun damage (and, potentially, injury to the gunner), Gatling no doubt recognized the need to redesign the system.

Model 1895

The Model 1895 Gatling gun was a slightly improved version of the Model 1893. Taking advantage of recent metallurgy improvements, one of the upgrades consisted of making some of the gun's internal operating components from a new bronze alloy to reduce wear. Having recognized that the Bruce feed system was clearly superior to all others, Gatling incorporated it on the Model 1895. Unlike earlier Gatling guns, on which the metal parts were left bare, the Model 1895's parts were either painted or blued. There were a few exceptions, as there are Model 1895 Gatlings in existence that have bare metal parts. Dr. Gatling probably incorporated the improvement after the Model 1895 entered production.

This model also had an improved armor configuration. The Model 1893's armor interfered with gun operation under certain conditions. On the Model 1895, the armor was redesigned to prevent interference.

Like the Model 1893, the Model 1895 was chambered for the .30/40 Krag cartridge. It was manufactured in five-, six-, and ten-barrel configurations.

Model 1900

The Model 1900 was identical to the Model 1895, with one important difference. For the first time on any Gatling gun, the bolts were interchangeable between barrels. This improvement resulted from manufacturing technology upgrades that allowed machinists to hold tighter tolerances on internal gun mechanism parts. On earlier Gatlings, the bolts had been fitted individually to each barrel.

Dr. Gatling also produced a special version of the Model 1900 for the U.S. Navy. Outwardly similar in appearance to the earlier Model 1883, the Model 1900 naval variant featured the fully enclosed bronze barrel jacket as well as selective crank placement.

Model 1903

At the turn of the century, the U.S. Army was experimenting with rifles captured from the Spanish during the War of 1898. These rifles, manufactured by Mauser in Germany, were probably the best the army had ever seen. The ordnance department was so impressed that it paid Mauser $200,000 for the rights to manufacture a similar weapon, which ultimately became the Model 1903 Springfield.

The army developed a cartridge for the Model 1903 Springfield that was similar to the captured Mausers' 7mm round. This cartridge did away with the .30/40 Krag's rimmed flange and kept the .30-caliber projectile. The resultant cartridge became the .30-03 Springfield (designating projectile diameter and year of introduction). The .30-03 cartridge and the bolt-action Springfield rifle that fired it became the standard-issue U.S. Army rifle.

In earlier years, Gatling guns were chambered in .50/70, .45/70, and .30/40, reflecting U.S. standard-issue weapons and cartridges of the era. In the same way, the Model 1903 Gatling was developed to fire the .30-03 cartridge. In all other respects, the Model 1903 was identical to the Model 1900.

Three years after the army adopted the Model 1903 and the .30-03 cartridge, the cartridge was modified slightly to improve its muzzle velocity. The result was the well-known .30-06, which replaced the .30-03 as the army's standard-issue cartridge. Existing Model 1903

Gatling guns were rechambered to fire the new round and designated Model 1903-06.

The End of an Era

The Model 1903-06 Gatling gun was the last of the early-era Gatlings. Under an agreement with the Gatling Gun Company, Colt built the guns for Gatling at its Hartford, Connecticut, facility until 1911. In 1911 the U.S. military declared the weapons obsolete. At the time, the decision was probably prudent, considering the arrival of newer and lighter fully automatic weapons (the Maxim machine gun, the Browning machine gun, etc.). The Gatling concept would lie dormant for nearly four decades, until advances in other war-fighting technologies created a need for very-high-rate-of-fire weapons.

CHAPTER 4

The Early Gatling
Guns in Action

*G*atling Parker was alive. He never felt more so than
when going into combat. His .30/40 Gatling guns,
blue steel and bronze cases glistening dully, were
ready. San Juan Hill was immediately ahead.
Theodore Roosevelt was somewhere off to the right.
Parker heard the bugler and the first shots, and the assault began. He
and his men pushed the Gatlings forward, firing as they advanced.
The sharp crack of the .30-caliber cartridges pierced the air—the sound
of one shot blending into another. The high pressure .30/40 sounded
even more powerful than the older and slower .45/70 it had replaced.
Before Gatling Parker realized it, eight minutes and 18,000 rounds
later, he stood at the top of San Juan Hill. Theodore Roosevelt stood next
to him, smiling slightly. Parker relaxed but for an instant, his breath-
ing still heavy from the uphill assault. He immediately began to turn
his Gatling around. His men did the same with their guns, realizing
that the inevitable counterattacks could only be minutes away.

Although Dr. Gatling patented his weapon in 1862, the Gatling gun
did not see widespread use in combat until much later. Though the
gun was invented primarily as a weapon to be offered to Union forces
during the Civil War, it saw only limited use during that conflict, and
the U.S. military was slow to adopt it.

With perfect hindsight, certain historians have claimed that the
Gatling gun could have brought the Civil War to a much speedier conclusion, kept Custer from being defeated at the Battle of the Little Big
Horn, and allowed the British Empire to expand more rapidly with
fewer lives lost. The basic premise of these and other impossible-to-
prove but interesting-to-ponder theories is that the Gatling met with
an inordinate share of stubborn opposition from ordnance officers
and governments of the era.

As a practical matter, the adoption of the Gatling gun probably
occurred at a pace no slower than that experienced by most other new
weapons. One must recognize that fielding any new weapon system,
even today, is a slow and methodical process under all but the most
extraordinary conditions. The Gatling was patented in 1862 and for-

mally adopted by the United States in 1866, a span of only four years. To put the situation into perspective, consider that it took more than ten years for the B-1 bomber to be adopted. In addition, finding a replacement for the .45 automatic pistol has taken decades.

The Civil War

As mentioned earlier, Col. James Ripley (the army's ordnance chief) was opposed to any new weapons for the Union forces, including the Gatling gun and a host of other weapons. Colonel Ripley argued that the army should retain a muzzle-loading infantryman's rifle, even though metallic cartridges had been invented almost twenty years earlier.

His opposition was not entirely without merit, as the army faced enormous logistics challenges supporting a seemingly infinite variety of weapons. He believed the army should standardize its armament with just a few weapons of demonstrated capabilities.

In 1862, the Gatling gun was neither standard nor combat-proven. Other early machine or volley-type guns offered terrible reliability, and frequent accidents gave these guns a well-deserved reputation for being hazardous. The first version of the Gatling gun (the Model 1862) was reliable and inaccurate. All machine guns of the era were plagued by similar (or worse) problems.

In addition, Dr. Gatling's rumored Southern sympathies probably further detracted from the gun's adoption by the North.

Gatling's promotional capabilities were equal to his mechanical genius, however. Despite numerous factors working against U.S. adoption of the then-new Gatling gun, it did see limited combat in the Civil War. The extent of its Civil War use is something time has largely obscured. The only confirmed combat deployment was in the Siege of Petersburg, which began in the summer of 1864 and continued under the command of General Butler until Lee surrendered at Appomattox in April 1865.

At that time, the capabilities of the machine gun as an infantry support weapon were not recognized. Butler (who apparently was a relatively free-thinking and wealthy general officer) purchased Dr. Gatling's twelve prototype Model 1862s for $12,000 following a sales demonstration, without bothering to ask the army for permission. During the Siege of Petersburg, he used the Gatlings to defend his fortified entrenchments. True to the military thinking of the day, the weapon was used in a defensive manner. According to some accounts, Butler personally manned the Gatlings on at least one occasion.

There are other unconfirmed reports of the Gatling gun being used in the Civil War. One of these was at the Battle of the Seven Pines, fought in Virginia from 31 May to 1 June 1862. Since the first Gatling gun was built in early 1862, it is conceivable. Another report holds that employees of the Gatling Gun Company, and on occasion even Dr. Gatling himself, took the Gatling gun into combat to give firsthand demonstrations of its effectiveness.

There are no confirmed instances of Gatling gun use by the navy during the Civil War, although individual navy commanders procured the weapons during the war. Admiral Dahlgren, chief of the navy's ordnance bureau, allowed procurement by commanders on an unofficial basis in 1863. Gatling Gun Company records indicate that some of the guns were sold and mounted on naval vessels. Gatling guns may have seen action on smaller boats used to patrol inland waterways.

One other example of Gatling gun use during the Civil War bears mention, if for no other reason than its being one of the few times these guns were directed at civilians. To meet the army manpower needs, the government implemented a draft by authority of the Conscription Act of 3 March 1863. For a variety of reasons this law was extremely unpopular, and riots erupted in several places. One of the worst occurred in New York City in July 1863. The *New York Times* supported the draft and criticized the rioters. Fearing an attack against the *Times* building, the editor and the owner of the newspaper manned two of the three Gatling guns emplaced to protect the building. Other staff members were armed with rifles. No attack materialized, probably as a result of the well-publicized display of force and a similarly well-publicized willingness to use it.

Westward Expansion

During the Civil War the U.S. Army failed to recognize the Gatling gun's potential as an infantry weapon, and Gatlings were utilized primarily as artillery pieces. This approach continued after the Civil War, when the army took Gatling guns into battle against the Indians. The navy did not use the Gatling during this period, as it saw essentially no combat until the end of the century.

Following the Civil War, the army focused on westward expansion, which naturally resulted in a series of conflicts with the American Indian. Although the army did not yet recognize the Gatling's capability as an infantry weapon for firing and maneuvering, it nonetheless recognized it as a very capable system. Each army detachment had several Gatlings as standard issue equipment. The key problems were that the army did not know how to best utilize the Gatling gun, and the limited military budgets of the era did not permit soldiers to practice enough to gain proficiency. Military thought held that the Gatling gun was to be classified either as an artillery piece or as a special weapon best suited for defending fixed fortifications (roads, bridges, or military installations). Most of the Gatling guns issued to the army during the period between the Civil

War and the Spanish-American War were used to defend military outposts on the Western frontier.

To be fair to the thinking of the period, however, one must recognize that the typical Gatling gun weighed about a thousand pounds. Failure to recognize the weapon as a "mobile" device is certainly understandable.

The army had an odd policy during much of this period regarding training and target practice. Although military outposts were located squarely in hostile Indian territory, the army economized by severely limiting (and in some cases preventing) training-related ammunition consumption. It was not at all uncommon for commanders to require soldiers to pay for training ammunition. This policy had a detrimental effect on marksmanship, and proficiency with the Gatling gun was particularly affected. When required to pay for ammunition that could be fired at over 750 shots per minute, soldiers tended not to practice too often. The army purchased close to five hundred Gatling guns during the Indian Wars, but most were never fired.

Buffalo Meat for Dinner

Surprisingly, the first firing of the Gatling gun during the westward expansion was not at Indians, but at buffalo. A herd of buffalo stampeded and charged a wagon train being escorted by the Seventh U.S. Cavalry. Two Gatling guns (the caliber is unknown, but they were almost certainly the Model 1866) were quickly brought to bear on the charging herd. They successfully repelled the buffalo, and in the process provided plenty of meat for the garrison.

Again, although the army procured hundreds of Gatling guns during the Indian War era, there are few documented instances of its use in combat. Although there are reasons the weapon did not see as much use as it might have, there were probably numerous combat engagements that were simply never recorded.

General Miles in West Texas

The first documented use of the Gatling gun against the Indians was in 1874, when it played a prominent role in three battles. The first was between an army expedition led by Col. (later Maj. Gen.) Nelson A. Miles and a group of Cheyenne, Comanche, and Kiowa Indians. Miles was an interesting officer. He began his career by purchasing a commission during the Civil War. Despite his career's questionable beginning, he soon distinguished himself as an outstanding officer. He rose to brevet major general, and after the Civil War he became a full colonel in the regular army. Most other post-Civil War army officers were West Point graduates, and there was a fair amount of snobbery and prejudice against Miles' undistinguished military lineage. Prejudice notwithstanding, he was a man who could get the job done.

He demonstrated that fact when he pursued the Indians into a battle that led to their encounter with the Gatling gun.

Colonel Miles led his men more than 700 miles to make contact with the Indians, sometimes traveling more than 30 miles in a single day in 110-degree heat. The heat and lack of water led some of the soldiers to cut their veins and drink their own blood in an attempt to quench their thirst. It was under these conditions that Miles and his troops were attacked on 30 August 1874, in an area of west Texas called El Llano Estacado (the "staked plains"). About 250 Indians attacked Miles' expedition of 700 men.

Lt. James Pope, under Colonel Miles, commanded a battery of Gatling guns (probably Model 1874). Lieutenant Pope advanced with two of the guns to engage the Indians, resulting in a decisive reversal of the ambush.

The Miles expedition was one of five under the command of Gen. Philip Sheridan. One of the other five columns, led by Maj. William Redwood Price, also used Gatlings to defeat the Indians. Price's command had numerous encounters with hostile Arapaho, Kiowa, Comanche, and Cheyenne Indians, and two of his Gatling guns figured in at least some of these skirmishes. One of Price's officers later published an account of the battles in the *British Journal of the Royal Service Institution*:

"In the Autumn of last year two Gatlings were reported to have done splendid service in frequent encounters with the Redskins on the Western Frontier. On one of these occasions, Major Price, of the Eighth United States Cavalry, was attacked by six hundred or seven hundred Indians, and he used his Gatlings with such excellent effect as to quite demoralize and drive off his savage assailants."

Custer at the Little Big Horn

Much has been written about Gen. George Armstrong Custer's involvement with the Gatling gun and, in particular, his decision to leave behind a contingent of Gatlings offered to him before the Battle of the Little Big Horn in 1876. Several factors played a role in that decision.

Custer recognized the Gatling gun's advantages and had used the weapon in the 1874 Black Hills campaign. He also recognized the limitations of a thousand-pound weapon in a light cavalry unit.

Custer's decision should not be considered without an understanding of other circumstances surrounding him. Whatever else he might have been, George Armstrong Custer was a controversial man. He graduated from West Point at the bottom of his class, yet he rose from the rank of lieutenant to brigadier general in one year during the Civil War. At age twenty-three, he was the youngest general to ever serve in the military forces of the United States. Two years later, just before the Civil War ended, he had attained the rank of major general and had earned a reputation as a hard-driving, successful cavalry commander. He dropped back to the rank of captain when the war ended, but within in a year he was promoted to lieutenant colonel and took command of the Seventh Cavalry.

Custer had a fatal flaw, however. His ego was enormous. His hunger for fame was apparent in his professed desire to link his name "not only to the present but to future generations" (a goal he certainly achieved). In his quests for glory, Custer drove his men relentlessly, sometimes ordering them shot for desertion. He was known to disobey orders he regarded as too conservative or timid, and on one such occasion he incurred the wrath of President Ulysses S. Grant, who had him arrested. Grant intended to court-martial him, but Custer begged for a chance to lead his troops back into combat with the Indians, and Grant relented. It was this scenario that set the stage for the Battle of the Little Big Horn, where Custer was destined to meet the Sioux Indians for the last time.

He was assigned to an expedition led by Gen. Alfred H. Terry. Hungry for glory and a chance to clear his name, Custer was anxious to be the first to establish contact with the Indians. Terry was concerned that Custer might encounter a numerically superior force, and he offered assistance from the Sixth Cavalry. Custer turned the offer down, claiming the additional troops were unnecessary. General Terry also offered him a battery of Gatling guns, and Custer refused these too, on the grounds that they would slow his advance and were unusable in the difficult terrain surrounding the Little Big Horn.

The true reasons for Custer's refusals were buried with him. Those who claim he was willing to pay any price to be the first to engage the Indians (thereby claiming all glory for himself) may be right. Custer refused reinforcements from the Sixth Cavalry, and he did have an insatiable ego. His argument about the Gatlings slowing his advance could have been an invention, since he was known to have taken an iron stove on other wilderness campaigns.

On the other hand, Custer's decision may have been tactically sound. Earlier during the same expedition, Lt. William Hale Low (commander of the Gatling battery offered to Custer) had difficulty keeping up with the cavalry due to the rough terrain. In some situations, the Gatlings had to be lowered by rope from steep hills. On at least one occasion Lieutenant Low and his Gatlings were lost during a night operation. Even if personal glory drove Custer's decision to leave the Gatlings behind, the decision is certainly supportable from a strictly military standpoint.

Newspaper accounts of the era and more recent discussions of Custer's decision to leave the Gatlings behind suggest that the 261 soldiers killed at the Little Big Horn might have been victorious had Custer taken the Gatlings. This could be true, but only because the guns could have slowed Custer's advance to the point that he might not have engaged the Sioux at all (or if he did, a slower advance would have kept him close to readily available reinforcements). Even if Custer had taken the Gatlings, one can only wonder if 261 men and two or three Gatling guns could have fought off the 2,500 Sioux warriors they met that day.

One other controversy surrounds Custer's association with the Gatlings during the campaign that ultimately led to his death. Many references state that the guns in Lieutenant Low's battery were .45/70 Gatlings. While the .45/70 was the standard infantry cartridge at the time, and the newer Model 1874 Gatling gun had been procured by the army in that caliber, the guns Custer turned down were not chambered for the .45/70. The preponderance of evidence, including diary accounts by members of the Terry expedition, shows the guns were .50-caliber. The model is unknown, but the Gatlings could have been either Model 1866 or Model 1871. In a small way, this seemingly insignificant fact further fueled the controversy. Had the lighter and more mobile Model 1874 been available to him, Custer might have taken the guns along.

The Nez Percé Campaign

The next recorded instance of the Gatling gun being used in combat against the Indians was in 1877. Through the summer and fall of that year, a small band of Nez Percé Indians traveled more than 1,700 miles in an attempt to escape the army and find a place to live. The U.S. government wanted land in the northwestern part of the Nez Percé territory. Chief Joseph, leader of the Nez Percé, stubbornly but politely refused to sign a treaty forfeiting his tribe's land. The Bureau of Indian Affairs found this to be an intolerable arrangement and asked in 1877 to have the army remove the Indians. Army lawyers concluded that the Nez Percé were the rightful owners, but Gen. O.O. Howard was ordered to carry out the bureau's request.

General Howard gave the Nez Percé thirty days to vacate their home and move to the reservation. Amazingly, and largely as a result of his influence over the Nez Percé and his love for peace, Chief Joseph convinced the Nez Percé to comply with the request. For some of them, though, the humiliation was too extreme. A small band of renegades struck out from the main party and killed four white settlers. In a second raid, the same band killed fourteen more whites.

The army's reaction was predictable, even though it was widely recognized that the renegades were but a small group (and that they had acted against Chief Joseph's wishes). A cavalry unit was directed to attack the Nez Percé, which they did. To General Howard's profound shock, the army was soundly defeated. Howard then sent a small cavalry unit to engage a small group of Nez Percé. A soldier killed a child during the attack, setting the tone for the events that followed.

The cavalry then opened fire with the Gatling gun, but most of the Indians had slipped away. The soldiers responded by burning the village. They continued in this manner, suffering small defeats and meaningless victories.

Meanwhile, the peace-loving Chief Joseph proved to be a brilliant cavalry tactician and guerrilla fighter. During a series of battles that covered 1,700 miles and lasted for several months, the Nez Percé continued to elude or defeat the pursuing soldiers.

The Gatling
Gun: 19th
Century
Machine Gun
to 21st
Century
Vulcan

38

On 11 July 1877, General Howard led six hundred men in a surprise attack on the encamped Nez Percé at Clearwater Ridge. General Howard used two Gatling guns and a cannon in the attack, but the Indians fought off the soldiers, and the army regrouped in a tight circle. Then Chief Joseph's force of less than one hundred Indians dug into fortified positions around the six hundred soldiers and put the army under siege. The army responded with Gatling gun and cannon fire, but they were pinned down for the rest of the day and through the night. The following morning, the remaining Nez Percé warriors withdrew (most of the other Indians left during the night). As the few remaining Nez Percé left, the army fired at them with the Gatlings. An officer in General Howard's command wrote that none of the Indians were hit (nonetheless, a *New York Times* article written four days later stated that the Gatling guns had driven off the Indians).

For the army, the experience was humiliating. Among other things, it demonstrated it did not know how to employ machine guns in either offensive or defensive actions. Had such tactics been developed, Howard's initial offensive might have been successful. Had the overlapping fields of fire used by today's infantry forces been considered, the Nez Percé would not have been able to surround and then lay siege to a numerically superior force. But such principles of machine gun employment would not be developed for another two decades.

Chief Joseph fought against Gatling guns one more time, in the final battle of the campaign. General Howard had signaled ahead for reinforcements to block the Indians' escape into Canada. General Miles obliged and was waiting for the now pitifully small band of Nez Percé in the Bear Paw Mountains, just 40 miles from the Canadian border. Miles had six hundred men, a Gatling, and a cannon. The fighting lasted for five days, with the Indians and the army both suffering heavy losses. On 5 October 1877, Chief Joseph surrendered.

The Bannock and Shoshone Campaigns

The last recorded use of Gatling guns in the Indian Wars is also the most well documented. James Henry Parker, who was to become the

United States' most knowledgeable machine gun tactician (and who later wrote a book on the subject based on his experiences with Gatling guns in the Spanish-American War) recorded the use of the Gatling gun against the Bannock and Shoshone Indians in 1878.

The army had forced the Bannock Indians to give up their land in what is now Oregon. With a small band of Shoshones (who were not normally hostile), the Bannocks left their reservation and attacked several cattle ranchers and other settlers. The army responded with the First Cavalry. The expedition had three .45/70 Gatling guns (based on the date and the caliber, they were almost certainly Model 1874s). When the cavalry engaged the Indians, the soldiers soon found themselves under heavy fire. Once the army positioned the Gatling guns on high ground to the right of the Indians, though, the heavy machine gun fire forced the Indians to retreat. In Parker's 1899 book, *Tactical Organization and Uses of Machine Guns in the Field*, he wrote:

"To gain a flank and pour in a sharp and unexpected fire upon the enemy is usually a decisive maneuver, and one particularly adapted to these guns. One can hardly argue. The effects of being surprised by a fusillade of Gatling fire can only be described as debilitating."

The Spanish-American War

The first time the United States used Gatling guns to fight the armed forces of another nation was in 1898 against Spain on the island of Cuba.

The Spanish-American War was not the first time Cubans heard Gatlings fired in anger. Three decades earlier, Cuban patriots had risen up against the Spanish government, and it took ten years (1868 to 1878) for the Spaniards to defeat the rebels. Spain ordered forty-six Camel Gatling guns in their standard .43 Spanish cartridge in December 1873.

There is no evidence to suggest that the Spanish ever used any of their Camel guns against the United States during the Spanish-American War, and except for the persistence of a visionary infantry officer, the United States might not have used its Gatlings, either.

Lt. John Henry Parker, a graduate of the U.S. Military Academy, was assigned to the invasion force sent to free Cuba. Parker recognized the Gatling gun's potential and asked to form a special unit armed with the weapons. His commander refused his request. Parker was not deterred, and he carried his request to the unit's commanding general. Gen. Joe Wheeler listened to Parker's ideas for using the Gatling in battle. Parker explained that he believed the military had not yet recognized the potential the Gatling had as an assault weapon. Parker developed the fire-and-maneuver principle for machine guns in the assault, a concept that infantry units rely on to this day. A heavy volume of machine gun fire is used to suppress the enemy while friendly troops move forward. Once the friendly troops have advanced, they lay down a wall of machine gun fire and the other Gatling-armed unit advances. The idea is to leapfrog in this manner until the target is overwhelmed.

Wheeler was impressed with both the idea and with Parker. He ordered Parker to organize a battery of Gatlings and test his ideas on the Cuban battlefield. According to conflicting historical accounts, Parker's detachment consisted of either four, five, or eight Gatling guns. The guns were chambered for the .30/40 Krag cartridge, the U.S. infantry standard at that time. Photos of Parker's detachment show that the guns were Model 1895s.

Parker's Gatling exploits became legendary after he participated in Theodore Roosevelt's charge up San Juan Hill. The Gatlings kept up a continuous volume of fire during the assault, allowing the United States to capture the Spanish position at the top in only eight and one-half minutes. During that time, the three Gatlings used fired more than 18,000 rounds. Once the U.S. troops were at the top, Parker turned his Gatlings around and successfully defended the hilltop against two Spanish counterattacks.

From that point on, Gatling guns became an indispensable part of every U.S. infantry and cavalry unit. Theodore Roosevelt expressed this clearly in his preface to Parker's book *The Gatlings at Santiago*:

"From thence on, Parker's Gatlings were our inseparable companions throughout the siege. When we dug our trenches, he took off the wheels of his guns and put them in the trenches. His men and ours slept in the same bomb-proofs and with one another whenever either side got a supply of beans or coffee and sugar. At no hour of the day or night was Parker anywhere but where we wished him to be, in the event of an attack. If a troop of my regiment was sent off to guard some road or some break in the lines, we were almost certain to get Parker to send a Gatling along, and, whether the charge was made by day or night, the Gatling went."

As a result of his success at Santiago, Parker was commissioned by the army to develop tactical doctrine for the employment of machine guns by the infantry. For the first time since the invention of the Gatling gun in 1862, the military recognized that it was an infantry weapon. Parker was the man who not only recognized and fully exploited the capability of the Gatling gun, but who paved the way for modern machine gun and infantry tactics. For the rest of his life he was known as "Gatling" Parker.

Action in the Philippines

Around the time the war was ending in Cuba, the United States found itself being drawn into combat in the Philippines. This time, the United States fought insurgents protesting U.S. rule of the

Philippine Islands, which had come about as a result of the Spanish-American War.

Up to this point there had been no recorded combat use of Gatling guns by the U.S. Navy. Although most ships were equipped with Gatlings, the navy had seen little opportunity to use them. That changed with the Philippine Insurrection. While the Gatlings were too cumbersome for army infantry units to use in the thick jungle terrain, the navy mounted Gatlings on its boats and, on at least two occasions, put them to excellent use.

The first action occurred when a Gatling-equipped gunboat answered shore-based rebel gunfire. The Gatlings quickly neutralized the rebel position. The same gunboat later killed several hundred rebels hiding in vegetation along the banks.

Incredibly, old Model 1865 Gatlings were used, and to make matters worse, they had never been modified to correct a timing problem (see Chapter 3) that occasionally resulted in their firing into the front of their frames. Several American sailors were injured as a result of timing failures. General Wheeler was incensed at the deployment of obsolete Gatlings. He threatened an investigation and promised to pursue legislation to buy more of the newer Gatling guns.

Service with Other Nations

Once the U.S. military had accepted the Gatling gun, the services of nearly every other nation in the world soon adopted it. This included Egypt, Morocco, China, Japan, most of Europe, most of South America, Russia, and Turkey.

Russia was the first foreign power to adopt the Gatling gun, bringing it into its arsenal in 1867, just one year after the United States formally adopted the weapon. Chambered for the .42 Russian infantry cartridge, the first Russian Gatlings were manufactured under the personal supervision of Colonel (later General) Gorloff of the Imperial Russian Artillery. These guns were of better quality than those sold to the United States, as they were made of stronger metals and had a finer finish. The Russians used their Gatlings in the Russo-Turkish War of 1877. The Turks had also equipped themselves with Gatlings built under license in Europe. The conflict is noteworthy in that it was the first known instance of two opposing forces being equipped with Gatling guns. The key battle of this war was fought in Plevna, a town in northern Bulgaria. During the battle, the Russians used their Gatlings primarily for defending bridges and roads at night, which showed that they were about as far along in their appreciation of machine gun tactics as the United States had been before the Spanish-American War.

France did not formally adopt the Gatling gun, choosing instead to equip its forces with the Mitrailleuse, a multibarreled volley gun.

Nonetheless, France was one of the first nations outside the United States to use the Gatling gun in combat. During the Franco-Prussian War of 1870-1871, most of the French Mitrailleuse weapons were captured. The French then purchased Gatling guns as replacements and used them to defend the town of Le Mans against the Germans.

England was one of the last major powers in Europe to adopt the Gatling gun, waiting until 1874. Once the British army and navy were equipped with Gatlings, though, they put them to good use. Most historians agree that the Gatling gun saw more combat with the British than with any other nation. Some have gone so far as to say that the British colonized the uncivilized world with the Gatling gun. While the last statement may be exaggerated, the British did use the Gatling extensively during their empire-building in Africa, South America, and the Middle East. The British brought two Gatling guns to western Africa in 1873 and 1874 to fight the Ashanti tribe. The Gatlings saw almost no combat use there, except for one instance in which the British fired the weapons merely to demonstrate the Gatling's capability and British resolve. One native actually committed suicide after witnessing the demonstration, apparently recognizing the futility of further resistance. Four years later, in 1878, the British used Gatling guns against the Zulus with devastating effectiveness. In 1882 British marines equipped with Gatlings quelled anti-British riots in Alexandria (firing the guns over the rioters' heads was enough to convince them to go home). The British used Gatlings in further conflicts in Egypt and the Sudan with superior results. They even developed an armored train, which was equipped with three Gatling guns, for use in this campaign.

The British appreciation for the Gatling gun did not stop with its land forces. The navy also made good use of the weapon. The HMS *Shah* successfully engaged a rebel Peruvian ironclad in 1877. Accurate fire from a mast-mounted Gatling forced the more heavily armed Peruvian ironclad to withdraw.

In another naval encounter two years later (during the War of the Pacific), Chilean forces fought the same vessel the *Shah* had defeated. By this time the Peruvian ironclad was equipped with Gatling guns (the Peruvians apparently learned their lesson). The Chilean vessel was also armed with Gatlings, making this the first known instance of two Gatling-equipped ships engaging in combat. The armies of both Chile and Peru were also armed with Gatling guns.

The Canadians used Gatling guns in the Riel Rebellion of 1885, which pitted rebel troops led by Louis Riel and renegade Meti Indians against the Canadian government. The Canadian government commissioned Lt. Arthur Howard of the Connecticut National Guard to lead its Gatling battery against the rebels. Lieutenant Howard did so with noted success and later became a captain in the Canadian military. He was killed in action with the Canadians in Africa a few years later.

The Gatling
Gun: 19th
Century
Machine Gun
to 21st
Century
Vulcan

42

The End of the Early Gatling

By the end of the century, most of the nations of the world had declared their Gatlings obsolete. The new automatic weapons of Hiram Maxim and John Browning offered superior performance with less weight, and they eliminated the need for manual cranking.

The United States waited until 1911 to declare its Gatling guns obsolete. Even then, nearly every U.S. military installation had a contingent of Gatling guns. In World War I, the United States even printed a manual for the "obsolete" Gatling.

There are intriguing reports of unusual use of the Gatling gun in later conflicts. For instance, the United States used the Gatling in the China Relief Expedition of 1900, and there is even a report of Red Chinese troops using Gatlings during the Korean War.

The declarations of governments around the world notwithstanding, the Gatling concept refused to die. Though the idea behind Dr. Gatling's invention would essentially lie dormant for almost forty years, its revival would have a profound effect—one that would make its presence felt in military weapons technology for years to come.

CHAPTER 5

Early Production
History

T he Russian colonel sat across the table, studying his
American negotiating opponent. "Dr. Gatling is a wor-
thy adversary," thought the Russian. "Shrewd, poker-
faced, but honest. He would have made a good Russian
officer." Russia wanted the seventy Gatling guns, and
the terms seemed reasonable, but still the American held out. "What
could he want?" the Russian wondered.

Dr. Gatling similarly studied his Russian adversary. He knew the
Russians would only buy a few weapons before they took the idea and
started producing the weapons themselves. The Russian colonel had
been into every corner of Gatling's factory, learning every detail of the
manufacturing process. Gatling didn't really want to sell the Russians
any of his guns. But he knew that if he didn't they would simply buy
one from one of the many other nations about to be armed with
Gatlings and then reverse-engineer it. "I either sell them a quantity of
the guns now," Gatling thought, "or I don't sell them any."

"The price is adequate, but only for larger quantities," Dr. Gatling
finally said. "I'll sell one hundred Gatling guns at the same price per gun.
We also wish to extend another option to your nation. The Gatling Gun
Company is prepared to offer a manufacturing license to the Imperial
Russian Army in consideration for the larger quantity of guns ordered."

The Russian looked at Dr. Gatling and smiled. After a brief pause,
so did Dr. Gatling. Each realized he had outwitted the other.

Early Gatling guns were manufactured from 1861 to 1911, both in
the United States and abroad. During this period, numerous models
were developed, and considering the variations in caliber, carriage,
number of barrels, and barrel length, several hundred distinct types of
Gatlings can be identified. The guns were manufactured in the United
States, Russia, Austria, and England. The Gatling gun's production history is perhaps as interesting as its combat use.

U.S. Production
The first prototypes of the Model 1862 Gatling, built in Indianapolis in late 1861 or early 1862, were used strictly for demonstration

The Gatling
Gun: 19th
Century
Machine Gun
to 21st
Century
Vulcan

46

purposes. Once Dr. Gatling had generated enough interest in his invention, he contracted Miles H. Greenwood and Company to build six of the Model 1862s. Greenwood, located in Cincinnati, was engaged almost exclusively in manufacturing Union war materiel and had been sabotaged several times by Confederate sympathizers. The saboteurs struck again as Dr. Gatling's guns were in production, and the weapons were lost in a fire.

Gatling found a new financial backer and in 1862 contracted the Cincinnati Type Foundry Works to build thirteen guns identical to those destroyed in the fire. Gatling and several business associates demonstrated the guns to several military officers, and Gen. Benjamin Butler was so impressed that he bought twelve of the thirteen with his own money. These were the first Gatling guns sold to the military (although the sale was unofficial).

Dr. Gatling also had an improved version of the Model 1862 built, although no manufacturing records exist for it or the prototype of the Model 1865s. The Cincinnati Type Foundry Works probably built both sets of guns.

Impressed with the Model 1865 during its official army trials, the army asked Dr. Gatling to build eight more in the giant 1-inch caliber. He turned to the Cooper Fire Arms Company of Philadelphia, which had a reputation for building high-quality small-percussion revolvers. The eight Gatlings Cooper manufactured performed accordingly, and the army ordered one hundred Gatling guns.

Since a bigger machine shop was needed to meet the production requirements, Gatling turned to Colt's Patent Fire Arms Company in Hartford, Connecticut, beginning a relationship that would last almost fifty years. Colt delivered the first one hundred guns to the army in 1867, and it built all remaining Gatlings manufactured in the United States during the early era of the weapon's history.

The relationship between Colt and the Gatling Gun Company would prove to be profitable for both parties. Colt had fallen on hard times after the Civil War and was anxiously looking for new products. Rollin White had patented metallic cartridge revolvers (Colt had turned down an opportunity to buy the patent), and Colt's percussion revolvers were no longer competitive. To make matters worse, the Colt plant had very nearly burned to the ground during an 1864 fire, and the company was hurt financially by the costs of rebuilding.

Colt turned to manufacturing anything in order to survive. In 1866, the list included sewing machines, printing presses, conductor's ticket punches, steam engines, and, of course, small arms. Under the circumstances, a lucrative government contract to build one hundred Gatling guns was particularly appealing.

While the Gatling Gun Company remained a separate business entity, it effectively became a part of the Colt organization. Dr. Gatling and his family moved to Hartford in 1870, and his company headquarters followed four years later. In 1897, the president of Colt also became the president of the Gatling Gun Company. At that time, Dr. Gatling was seventy-nine years old and was probably ready to step down as the chief executive of the world's most successful machine gun company. He retained 10 percent of the stock, however. Interestingly, Daniel B. Wesson (of the Smith & Wesson Company) owned about 6 percent of the Gatling Gun Company. Smith & Wesson was one of Colt's major competitors at the time and still is today.

More than a thousand Gatling guns were built in the United States, all but the first few by Colt. About 725 were purchased by the U.S. Army, which appears to have procured the weapon steadily throughout its entire production history. Several were sold to the U.S. Navy, although Gatling's navy procurement records were not as thorough. The remaining U.S.-built Gatlings were sold to civilian agencies (police departments, prisons, etc.) and foreign governments. Most of the Gatling guns procured by foreign governments, though, were manufactured abroad.

Foreign Gatling Gun Production

Immediately after the Civil War, Russia purchased two Model 1862 Gatlings for testing. The Russians were impressed. They sent Colonel Gorloff of the Imperial Russian Artillery to Hartford, initiating talks aimed at procuring a quantity of improved Gatling guns for Russia. Russia ordered twenty Model 1866 Gatlings chambered for its .42-caliber infantry cartridge.

When the Russians placed a second order for seventy Gatling guns, Dr. Gatling offered them a manufacturing license if they would increase their order to one hundred. They happily obliged. After that, all Russian Gatlings were built in Russia. The total number the Russians built is unknown, but it must have been significant. As early as 1876, they had four hundred Gatlings in their arsenals.

The E.A. Paget Company of Austria also manufactured Gatling guns for a brief period. Paget built Gatlings (under license to the Gatling Gun Company) for Turkey, which was engaged in a centuries-old conflict with Russia. Turkey knew Russia had Gatlings, and it did not want to be outgunned. The Turks ordered two hundred Gatling guns in 1870. These went to the Turkish army. The Turkish navy followed with an order for thirty Gatlings.

Dr. Gatling transferred both orders to Paget in Vienna. The Gatling Gun Company had met with Paget a year earlier, and apparently this was the first instance in which geography made such an arrangement feasible. Unlike the Russians, Paget had to pay a royalty on each Gatling gun it manufactured. The Austrians built Gatlings of inferior quality, and the Paget organization's problems were compounded by financial difficulties. Not wishing to be tied to a company that could tarnish the Gatling name, Dr. Gatling dissolved the relationship in 1871.

In 1869, the Gatling Gun Company granted a manufacturing and sales license to Sir William G. Armstrong and Company in England, which he renewed in 1881. Both Gatling and Armstrong profited from extensive British use of the Gatling gun. The Armstrong Company's total production of Gatling guns is unknown, but it probably numbered in the thousands. Armstrong also sold many Gatlings to other nations in whatever caliber was desired. Some were quite unusual, including one that fired a 3 1/4-ounce .65- caliber bullet and another that fired a 4 1/2-ounce .75-caliber bullet.

In 1888, Frederick C. Penfield, another British Gatling gun manufacturer, bought the European patent rights for $100,000 and Gatling's European subsidiary for $50,000. Under the terms of this arrangement, Penfield paid the Gatling Gun Company a $100 royalty for each gun manufactured. Within a year, though, Penfield violated the agreement by selling several Gatling guns to Chile and failing to pay the royalties. As a result of this and other problems, the arrangement was liquidated in 1890.

After 1890, British Gatling gun manufacturing history grows hazy. Accles and a fellow by the name of Grenfell were the successors to the arrangement with Penfield. Accles was a former employee of the American Gatling Gun Company (he invented the feed system that bore his name). He also invented an improved version of the Gatling gun that he named the Accles gun. About this time, the Maxim machine gun was eclipsing all manually operated machine guns, which doomed the Accles weapon to fail commercially and militarily.

Gatling Gun Production Ends

Most of the nations equipped with Gatling guns stopped using them around the turn of the century. The U.S. Army waited until 1911 to declare the Gatling obsolete, and in that year Colt discontinued production. The weapon would remain out of production for forty years, until world events ushered in new firepower requirements that only the Gatling gun could meet.

CHAPTER 6

A Prelude to the Future

*T*he navy engineers studied the modified Gatling gun, realizing that the electrically powered weapon offered amazing possibilities. A civilian engineer from the company that had modified the weapon stood by, ready to answer any questions that the navy might ask. The ten-barreled Gatling glistened dully, its bronze casing diffusing the bright sunlight. An unusual electric motor was mounted on the left side of the receiver, with copper wire coils that stood out in the morning light. The civilian engineer walked over to the weapon, aligned the sights at a distant target, and closed the switch with his thumb. The Gatling gun sounded unlike anything the ordnance engineers had ever heard. It roared rather than barking out the staccato pops characteristic of hand-cranked Gatlings. In less than a few seconds it had fired more than a hundred rounds. Smoke drifted up slowly as the roar reverberated off the distant hills.

Electric motors became practical near the end of the nineteenth century. Initial designs were inefficient and low in power, but as the electric motor improved, engineers found many new applications. One of these was the Gatling gun.

The U.S. Navy and the Crocker-Wheeler Motor Company pioneered in this area, developing the first version of an electrically powered Gatling gun in 1890. The 15 November 1890 edition of *Scientific American* carried a front-page story about the navy's Crocker-Wheeler electrically powered Gatling gun, which stated:

"The Crocker-Wheeler Motor Company, of this city, were invited by the U.S. Navy Department to arrange an electric firing mechanism for the Gatling gun. Several requirements had to be kept in mind in producing the design. The apparatus had to be attached to the barrel of the gun so as to move with it. It had to be out of the sighting line, and it was necessary to dispose of it so as not to interfere with elevation or depression of the gun. The motor finally had to be adopted for operation by the electric lighting plants as installed upon the ships of war."

The Navy Crocker-Wheeler electric Gatling gun could fire at a rate of 1,500 RPM, the highest rate of fire ever achieved at the time (although earlier versions of manually fired Gatlings could fire short bursts at 1,250 RPM).

The concept of a motor-driven gun system was revolutionary, and the Crocker-Wheeler electric Gatling gun represented a quantum leap forward in weapons technology. Shortly after the navy began working with Crocker-Wheeler, Dr. Gatling started developing his version of an electric Gatling gun. His first design attained a firing rate of 1,500 RPM, matching that of the Crocker-Wheeler gun. Dr. Gatling improved his design over the next two years and ultimately built a gun that could fire at the phenomenal rate of 3,000 RPM (which he patented in 1893).

In some respects, Dr. Gatling's gun was similar to the navy's. Both had ten barrels chambered for the .30/40 Krag cartridge, both were driven by electric motors, and both had bronze jackets. But there were significant differences as well. The Gatling design contained the electric motor inside the bronze breech housing (for a totally bronze-encased gun), while the Crocker-Wheeler design mounted the motor externally. The Gatling design totally eliminated the hand crank, while the Crocker-Wheeler retained it as a backup. The Gatling design was also water-cooled (the only Gatling ever known to have this feature). Dr. Gatling believed that water-cooling would be needed to control the heat generated when firing at 3,000 shots per minute.

Unfortunately, both Gatling and the navy terminated further development of the electrically powered Gatling gun. There were two reasons for this.

One was the advent of the gas-operated Maxim machine gun, which required neither manual cranking nor electrical power. Although the Maxim's rate of fire (well under 1,000 RPM) was much lower than that of the electric Gatling gun, the Maxim was considerably lighter, making it attractive to both the army and the navy. The navy could have tolerated the added weight and complexity of an electric Gatling gun, as shipboard mounting eliminated the need for easy transportability, and power was readily available. The army, however, required a lighter weapon that did not require exter-

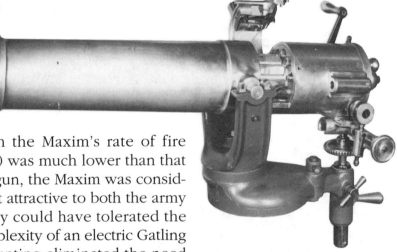

Figure 12. A Model 1879 .45/70 Gatling gun on a naval mount, and a modern electrically driven 20mm M-61 Vulcan Gatling gun.

nal power, and as a result, it never expressed an interest in the electrically powered Gatling gun.

The other reason for terminating development was that in the 1890s there simply was no need for the electrically powered Gatling gun's extremely high rate of fire, which was its principal advantage. In fact, when viewed from the logistical perspective of the era, the high rate of fire was a serious disadvantage. Large quantities of ammunition would be required to feed such a weapon, and gunners would have little time to adjust fire before even a short burst emptied the gun. In another forty years there would be a requirement for a gun that could fire at 3,000 shots or more per minute. And even then, not all of the technology would exist to solve the logistics and aiming problems (more on this in the next chapter).

By 1895 it was apparent that the gas-operated machine gun would eclipse the Gatling gun. In an effort to delay this, Colt employee Carl J. Ehbets developed and patented a means of converting the Gatling to gas operation. Each barrel of the Ehbets-modified Gatling gun had a small orifice near the muzzle. When the first round fired, some of the gas used to propel the bullet escaped through this orifice. The escaping gas actuated a spring-loaded lever, which was subsequently returned to its original position by the spring. In the process of returning to its original position, the lever actuated a ratchet mechanism. The ratchet mechanism indexed the next firing barrel into position, and another round fired. The operating mechanism in the breech of the gun was essentially the same as that of a manually cranked Gatling. The gas-operated Gatling gun still required manual cranking to touch off the first round, after which it would continue to fire in a fully automatic manner.

The gas-operated Gatling gun never appealed to the military during this early period. The need to hand-crank the gun to fire the first round was perhaps marginally acceptable, but it had the same disadvantages as the electrically powered Gatling. Compared to the Maxim, any version of the Gatling gun was simply too heavy. The weight problem was only aggravated by adding gas operation or electrical power. Interestingly enough, when General Electric developed a gas-operated Gatling gun nearly eighty years later, it faced the same problems—weight and the need to crank the gun to fire the first shot. (The modern version of the gas-operated Gatling gun did make it to production in the SUU-23/A gun pod, as will be explained in Chapter 14.)

Although no military force adopted these early electrically powered or gas-operated Gatlings, the ideas were decades ahead of their time. The problem was not that these inventions were poor solutions to a military requirement. Rather, the electrically powered and gas-operated Gatling guns were excellent solutions to a problem that did not yet exist. This would change with the advent of high-performance aircraft six decades later, when the need for guns with extremely high rates of fire would become evident.

7 Project Vulcan

A cool morning fog covered the airfield, and Hans von Ohain shivered. Ohain was cold, but his trembling was more the result of excitement than temperature. He looked at the strange aircraft—it had no propeller, and it seemed to project a combination of aggressiveness, muscularity, and speed. Several men spoke excitedly in German as they connected auxiliary power equipment to the experimental vehicle. Although unbelievable events were occurring in Germany almost daily, Ohain was oblivious to them. He had focused his efforts on developing the jet engine in the now ready-to-fly experimental Heinkel. For three years, he had worked incredibly long hours in a small shop in Warnemunde, ignoring the rest of the world. Ohain felt his heart race as the jet engine noise increased and the Heinkel began its takeoff roll. He knew the course of aviation history was about to be altered irrevocably.

On 7 August 1939, just four days before the start of World War II, a small group of scientists and engineers made history on small airfield deep in Nazi Germany. The Heinkel 178 flew for the first time, and in so doing, marked the advent of a new era in aviation. The Heinkel was the world's first jet-powered aircraft. With its first flight, the pace and direction of aeronautical development changed forever.

Developments in this area proceeded rapidly, and by 1944 both Germany and England had operational jet fighters. Germany's Messerschmitt Me 262 was capable of speeds approaching 600 miles per hour. England's Gloster Meteor was slower, but it easily outclassed existing propeller-driven aircraft. The United States had two prototype jet fighters (Bell's XP-59 Airacomet and Lockheed's F-80 Thunderjet), but neither achieved operational status during the war.

Evolving Combat Requirements

As World War II drew to a close, U.S. defense engineers recognized that the requirements for aircraft gun armament were changing. During the war, the .50-caliber Browning machine gun was the standard aircraft gun. The aircraft version of this weapon was essentially an adaptation of the ground-based machine gun. The cyclic rate of fire for the Browning had been pushed up to approximately 1,200 RPM, which was at the time considered to be the maximum practical limit. With the advent of jets, however, it became increasingly clear that the older .50-caliber guns were no longer adequate.

There were several reasons for this, but the predominant one was speed. Future encounters between aircraft could occur in an instant, with jet fighters charging each other at closing speeds exceeding 1,200 miles per hour. Similarly, jets attacking ground targets would have less time to locate and engage the enemy, as the time over the target would be but a fleeting instant. It became increasingly clear that something more like a shotgun than a machine gun would be needed. An aircraft-mounted shotgun would not be practical, but if the rate of fire of a machine gun could be made high enough, a machine gun burst could become, in effect, a shot pattern.

Another reason for replacing the .50-caliber machine gun was its poor lethality. Newer aircraft and many ground targets were becoming harder to kill. They were less vulnerable to gun-inflicted damage from the old .50-caliber solid projectiles. This was particularly true for ground targets, which increasingly utilized armor protection. Even certain aircraft had armor plating around the pilot.

In 1945 the Army Air Corps and the small arms branch of the army ordnance research and development service recognized this problem and issued a list of new requirements for aircraft machine guns. They specified that the new machine gun had to be more powerful than the old .50-caliber Browning and have a rate of fire of at least 1,250 RPM. Curiously, the rate-of-fire requirement was only marginally higher than that of the Browning machine gun. Perhaps the army planners did not believe significantly higher rates of fire were technically feasible. The army artillery branch also became interested in this effort, as they needed a more powerful weapon for antiaircraft applications.

The army recognized several options for increasing aircraft armament lethality. One approach was to increase projectile weight, velocity, or both. Another approach was to add an explosive charge to the projectile. There were trade-offs between the two approaches. Adding explosive to the projectile would put more energy on the target, but an explosive projectile wasn't feasible in a smaller round (there wasn't room to add enough explosive to attain desired lethality levels). Smaller projectiles could attain higher velocities, though, and therefore impart more energy to the target.

The army initially selected a new .60-caliber cartridge that used the 20mm case necked down to accept the .60-caliber projectile (.60 inch is approximately equal to 14mm). Army ordnance engineers believed the higher muzzle velocity of the .60-caliber projectile would provide the necessary increase in lethality.

The army examined several design approaches for the new gun.

One school of thought concentrated on developing a very-high-rate-of-fire machine gun. The concept called for having several bullets in one barrel at the same time. This approach failed. During development testing, the barrel literally separated from the gun and flew downrange. The gun's design could have been strengthened to prevent this, but the engineers recognized that the concept was doomed for other reasons. The barrel of such a weapon would heat and wear rapidly, thus rendering it useless.

Another approach called for a revolver-type weapon, based in part on a German World War II design. This gun suffered from the same problems normally associated with revolvers (gas loss at the chamber-to-barrel interface and unacceptably large dispersion induced by the barrel's forcing cone). As a single-barreled weapon similar to the very high rate of fire machine gun described above, it also suffered from excessive barrel heating and wear.

The Gatling Gun Reemerges

Based on the above, the army concluded that some kind of externally powered, multibarreled weapon capable of very high firing rates was needed. Ordnance engineers concluded that the Gatling gun concept was probably the best design approach. This was based on the firing rate of 3,000 RPM that Dr. Gatling had achieved with an electrically powered version of his gun (see Chapter 6). In addition, the Gatling approach could solve many of the problems that plagued the very-high-rate-of-fire machine gun and revolver designs. Barrel heating and the subsequent high wear rates would no longer be problems, as the Gatling used multiple barrels. Gas leakage, which had been a problem on the revolver-based gun, would be overcome by the Gatling's integral barrels and chambers. The engineers also recognized that accuracy would be much better due to the Gatling's integral barrel and chamber design (which eliminated the forcing-cone-induced accuracy problems associated with revolver-based weapons).

The Gatling approach offered another significant advantage. The Gatling gun was externally powered, meaning each round was not dependent on the successful functioning of the preceding round. If a round failed to fire in a Gatling gun, it was mechanically extracted and ejected. The gun would continue to operate. This would result in a more reliable weapon, which would increase combat effectiveness.

Thirty-four years after the army had officially declared the Gatling gun obsolete (in 1911), with the impetus of jet aircraft that could fly near the speed of sound, the Gatling gun concept was pulled out of retirement. The army's ordnance research and development service recommended pursuing a design based on the Gatling gun, and in early 1945 it awarded a contract to Johnson Automatics, Inc.

Johnson Automatics was a small weapons development company

headed by Melvin Johnson, a former U.S. Marine Corps officer best known for his invention of the Johnson light machine gun and the Johnson semiautomatic rifle. About fifty thousand of these weapons were delivered during World War II. Johnson also developed a 20mm aircraft gun for the navy, and he no doubt recognized the potential market for a new aircraft gun system.

History Repeats Itself

Johnson had a difficult time locating a Gatling gun in serviceable condition, but he persisted and finally found one in New York City. The gun was a Model 1883 with ten bronze-encased barrels chambered for the .45/70 cartridge. It had an Accles feed system.

Rather than using the design approaches pursued earlier by Dr. Gatling and the navy on their electrically powered Gatlings (both of which used direct mechanical gear drives), Johnson connected an electric motor to the Gatling gun with a belt and pulley arrangement. Other than that, only a few modifications were made to the old Model 1883. The original bolts were replaced with ones of stronger steel, and an electric burst limiter was incorporated in the control circuitry.

Johnson's work was quite successful. The gun first fired in late 1945 at a rate of 3,000 RPM, duplicating Dr. Gatling's 1893 achievement. Subsequent refinements to the Johnson-modified Gatling ultimately brought the rate of fire up to 5,800 RPM, a staggeringly high number from a single weapon. Johnson submitted his technical report to the army early in 1946, recommending that the Gatling concept be pursued.

The General Electric Vulcan

The army followed Johnson's recommendation and in the summer of 1946 awarded a contract to General Electric's armament division in Burlington, Vermont. The project was named "Vulcan" in honor of the Roman god of fire and metalworking. Project Vulcan was to be a joint effort between the Army Air Force (the air force would not become a separate service until late 1947), the U.S. Army Department of Ordnance, and General Electric.

The contract awarded to General Electric contained several requirements for the new gun system. The contract specified a .60-caliber projectile (the cartridge discussed earlier), an overall gun length not exceeding 80 inches, and a total system weight not exceeding 100 pounds. The minimum rate of fire specified was 1,000 shots per minute (which was surprisingly low, considering the success Johnson had enjoyed a year earlier). The army believed that the .60 caliber was optimal for the intended application. Developmental work with .60-caliber guns would go on for several years, but the cartridge would ultimately be dropped (for reasons to be explained later).

General Electric completed the first prototype Vulcan in April

1949. The electrically powered gun, designated the T-45, had 779 parts and fired at a rate of 2,500 RPM. Later improvements increased the firing rate to 4,000, 5,000, and finally 6,000 shots per minute. Encouraged by the results, the U.S. Army and Air Force funded General Electric to build ten more T-45 Vulcans. These guns were subjected to extensive accuracy, reliability, and environmental tests, and in every case the results were extremely good.

The next step was to begin work on a production version of the Vulcan. General Electric built thirty-three production prototypes in late 1950 and early 1951. There were four versions built in three calibers. Two were for the .60 caliber (the T-45 discussed earlier and a shorter version designated as the T-62). A third version, designated the T-171, was chambered for the 20mm cartridge. The fourth, designated the T-150, was chambered for an experimental 27mm cartridge. Mechanically, all four guns were quite similar. All of the cartridges were based on the 20mm cartridge case (which was necked down for the .60 caliber and necked up for the 27mm projectiles).

The army subjected all of the guns to extensive testing at Aberdeen Proving Grounds and Springfield Armory. The results were impressive. All of the production prototypes could fire at rates in excess of 6,000 RPM. One gun that the army subjected to extreme reliability testing fired 75,000 rounds without a single failure. That may not sound like much for a gun capable of firing 6,000 RPM, but the fact that these guns generally fire in short bursts of 100 rounds or less should be taken into consideration (more on this in later chapters). As an interesting historical footnote, a Model 1873 Gatling gun underwent a similar test conducted by the U.S. Navy at Annapolis in 1873. In that test, the Gatling gun fired 100,000 rounds over a three-day period without any failures. During the 1873 test, the gun crew members poured water on the barrels to keep them from overheating! In both instances, the military discovered that the Gatling gun concept was quite reliable.

Based on the results of the testing, General Electric received a production contract for twenty-seven additional test and evaluation guns in 1952. The army specified six barrels, an overall length of 72 inches, an 11-inch diameter, either hydraulic or electric drive power, a weight of 300 pounds, and a minimum firing rate of 6,000 shots per minute.

The army also specified that the new guns be chambered for the 20mm cartridge. The war in Korea showed conclusively that the old .50-caliber Browning machine gun cartridges were grossly inferior to the 20mm in air-to-air combat. The army recognized that the .60 caliber was only a slight improvement over the .50 caliber (even though it had a significantly higher muzzle velocity).

The United States had four types of jets in Korea, and three of these (the Lockheed F-80 Shooting Star, the Republic Aviation F-84 Thunderjet, and the North American F-86 Sabre) were armed with the

.50-caliber machine gun. While these aircraft all did reasonably well in combat, American combat aviators were more impressed with the navy's F9F Panther armament.

The Panthers had four single-barreled 20mm cannon, and the lethality of 20mm guns was significantly better than that of the .50-caliber machine guns. The navy and the air force also knew that the North Korean MiG 15s were equipped with two 23mm guns and one 37mm cannon. The general feeling was that a significant increase in armament caliber and lethality would best serve U.S. needs.

U.S. military forces wanted the aerodynamic efficiency of a small-diameter projectile, but they also realized that a high-explosive warhead was required for adequate lethality. A .60-caliber projectile was too small to carry a high-explosive charge and its associated fuzing. The 20mm was the smallest diameter that could meet this requirement, and it became the logical choice, offering a sensible compromise between aerodynamic efficiency and explosive payload.

Testing of the Vulcans continued for four more years. In 1956, the test program culminated in the T-171 Vulcan being officially type-classified as the M61 Aircraft Cannon. The M61 and its derivatives became the standard U.S. aircraft gun.

From its beginnings during the Civil War, the Gatling gun had evolved into a state-of-the-art aircraft armament system. Modifications of the M61 have been adapted to air defense gun systems, close-in ship defense gun systems, ground saturation-fire gun systems, anti-tank gun systems, and even man-portable infantry weapons. The chapters to follow explore each of these in greater detail.

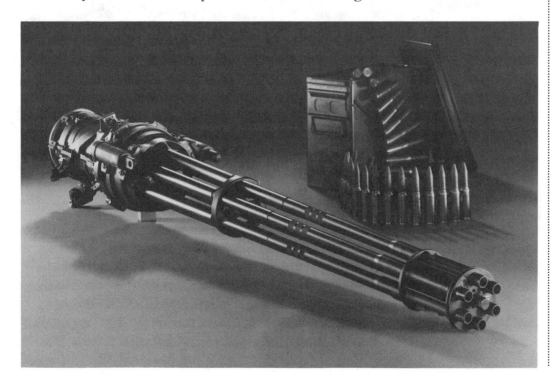

Figure 13. The M61 Vulcan cannon. The Vulcan cannon, based on the original Gatling gun concept, fires 20mm ammunition from six barrels. Firing rates can be as high as 6,000 shots per minute.

CHAPTER 8

20mm Vulcan Operation

Although the F-4's cockpit was air-conditioned, the pilot was perspiring profusely. At 300 feet above the jungle canopy, he knew that he was extremely susceptible to small-arms fire from the Vietcong forces known to be operating in the area. He also knew that in another minute, he would be across the Laotian border and into an area where enemy truck convoys routinely traveled the Ho Chi Minh Trail to deliver supplies to their comrades further south. Returning from a bombing run near the demilitarized zone (where he had successfully delivered eight Rockeye cluster munitions against a North Vietnamese position), he had heard the frantic call for air support from a Special Forces A-Team in Laos.

"Approaching your area," the pilot said into his mask. "Pop smoke to identify position."

"Popping smoke," came the reply from the Green Beret captain on the ground. As was customary, the ground commander did not identify the color. That would make it too easy for the enemy to deploy the same color smoke grenades to confuse the desperately needed air support. The pilot could hear the crackle of small-arms fire in the background of the ground transmission. He knew the Special Forces were taking heavy fire.

"I see blue," the pilot said.

"Roger that," the Green Beret officer responded. "Victor Charlie is 50 yards north of our location. Request twenty mike-mike suppression, put down from east to west."

"Out," was the pilot's only response, as he banked sharply and dropped to 100 feet. With his right hand, he flipped the master arm switch to the armed position and the joystick-mounted gun-camera switch to the gun position. He pulled the throttles back slightly with his left hand, letting the banked turn and reduced thrust drop his airspeed to an indicated 250 knots. He saw the blue smoke a half-mile ahead, slightly to his left. The sun created a little glare in the thousands of minute canopy scratches.

"It's show time," he said into the microphone. The pilot dropped the nose ever so slightly and squeezed the joystick trigger. He heard, or rather felt, a slight shudder as the mighty 20mm cannon belched out a *burst of 4,000 RPM high-explosive and tracer ammunition. He saw the rounds arc out, dispersing ever so slightly and then erupting in bursts of high explosive that were visible even through the thick jungle cover. He continued flying low, accelerating to minimize exposure to ground fire. "How's it look down there?" he said into the mask.*

"Like it should," he heard over the speaker from the Green Beret. "We estimate you just won the hearts and minds of at least an enemy platoon, possibly two platoons . . ."

The Gatling
Gun: 19th
Century
Machine Gun
to 21st
Century
Vulcan

60

The M61Al 20mm Vulcan is the foundation of the current family of modern Gatling guns manufactured by General Electric's Defense System Division in Burlington, Vermont. While the company offers numerous variants of the weapon (with several barrel, caliber, drive-power, and feed-system options), the 20mm Vulcan was its first production model and is still in production. The Vulcan's principles of operation formed the basis for all subsequent models, and therefore, it is a good starting point for any discussion of contemporary Gatling gun operation.

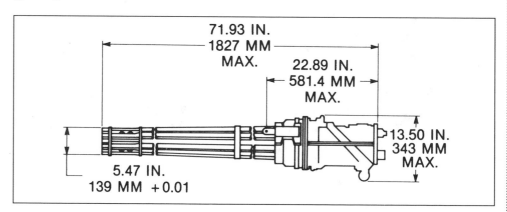

Figure 14. Specifications and other information on the General Electric M61A1 Vulcan cannon. Modern Gatling guns are manufactured by General Electric in Burlington, Vermont.

Characteristics

Type .... Externally powered 6-barrel Gatling
Length .... 73.4 inches (1864.4 mm)
Max. Diameter .... 13.5 inches (342.9 mm)
Power to Drive @ 4,000 spm .... 8 hp (6 kw)
Power to Drive @ 6,000 spm .... 20 hp (14.9 kw)
Rounds to First Scheduled Maintenance 30,000
Reliability .... 100,000 MRBF
Ammunition .... M50 Series
Muzzle Velocity .... 3,380 ft (1030 m)/sec
Rate of Fire .... Variable to 7,200 spm
Average Recoil Force:
    @ 4,000 spm .... 2,661 pounds (11.9 kn)
    @ 6,000 spm .... 3,818 pounds (17.1 kn)
Recoil Travel (Max.) .... 0.25 inch (6.35 mm)
Drive Type .... Hydraulic, electric, or pneumatic
Feed System Type .... Linked or linkless
Clearing Method .... Holdback or declutching
Dispersion (80% of rds. fired) .... 8 mils or 2.2 mils normal radial dispersion

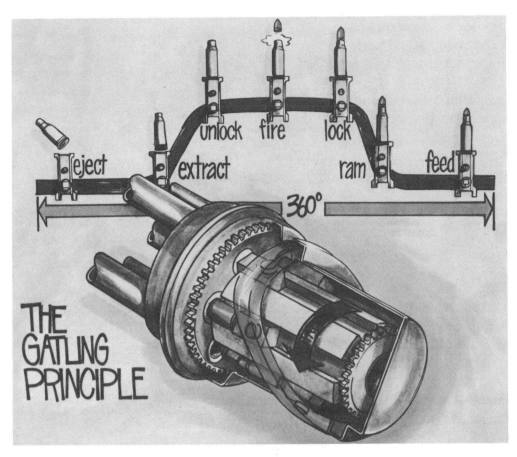

eject extract unlock fire lock ram feed

360°

THE GATLING PRINCIPLE

Amazingly, aside from expected differences in chambering, metallurgy, drive power, and other engineering advances, the principle of operation for modern Gatlings is hauntingly similar to that of the Model 1865 (the first Gatling to use metallic cartridges) discussed in Chapter 2.

Let's begin with a look at the modern gun's components and operational sequence. The M61A1 20mm Vulcan is shown in

Figure 15. An exploded view of the Vulcan showing the basic Gatling gun operating steps. Note the similarity to the original Gatling gun shown in Figure 5 (page 10).

Figure 14. An isometric drawing illustrating the Vulcan principle of operation is shown in Figure 15.

The Vulcan system consists of the following major subsystems and assemblies:

- the rotor
- the stationary rotor housing
- the rotating barrel cluster
- the drive unit (includes the two speeds)
- the feeder and ammunition handling system
- the recoil adaptors

Each of these is explained below.

The Rotor and Stationary Rotor Housing

Two portions of the 20mm Vulcan rotate when the gun is fired. The rotor and the barrel cluster spin as an assembly. The rotor, which is driven by the drive unit, contains six sets of tracks that spin with it. Each track has a bolt assembly that engages an elliptical cam path in the rotor housing. The cam path drives the bolts back and forth as the rotor rotates and the bolt follows the elliptical path.

When the rotor rotates within the rotor housing, the bolts perform essentially the same function as did those of the original

Gatling guns. The bolt assemblies engage the rim on each round as it is fed from the feeder and drive the round into the chambered position. A feature on the rotor housing then locks the bolt in the firing position.

As this is occurring, other features on the rotor housing cam path cock the firing pin within the bolt and then release it to form a very slight indentation on the cartridge primer. At this point, an electrical signal is sent to the bolt, which transmits the signal to the chambered 20mm round. The 20mm Vulcan ammunition is electrically primed, and this signal fires the round. (Note that the 20mm Vulcan is the only version of the modern Gatling to use electrically primed ammunition. All others, from the tiny 5.56mm version to the mighty 30mm GAU-8/A Avenger, use standard percussion priming.)

The next step in the firing sequence is to unlock the bolt (which is again actuated by a camming feature in the rotor housing). As the rotor continues to rotate, the rotor housing elliptical cam path forces the bolt rearward, which extracts the fired cartridge case. The extracted case encounters a fixed guide bar (mounted on the stationary rotor housing), which guides the spent case out of the rotor. In some versions of the Vulcan, the spent case is kept under positive control in the ammunition handling system and returned to the emptying ammunition storage drum; in others, it is simply dumped overboard.

The Rotating Barrel Cluster

The rotating barrel cluster consists of the guns, six barrels, a center barrel clamp, and the muzzle clamp. The six-barreled Vulcan is more or less the standard system; however, variants with three, four, and five barrels are available. The barrels have right-hand, gain-twist rifling (meaning as the 20mm projectile travels through the bore, it spins at a progressively faster rate in a right-hand direction).

The barrels are each attached to the rotor with an interrupted thread. After the muzzle clamp is removed (it is held in place by a single nut), the barrels can be removed by simply turning each 60 degrees in either direction and pulling it straight out. The life of the barrel cluster is 72,000 rounds (after the gun has fired 72,000 rounds, the barrels are all replaced), which means that each barrel has a life of 12,000 rounds. This is actually quite good, particularly when considered in light of the Vulcan's 3,380-fps muzzle velocity. Most small arms with comparable muzzle velocities have barrel lives of 3,000 to 5,000 rounds.

Practically speaking, it is essentially impossible to overheat the Vulcan's barrels. At the lower firing rates (typically 1,000 RPM), each barrel is firing about 170 shots per minute. The ammunition supply in all Vulcan applications (usually 300 to 1,000 rounds) is too small to allow the gun to heat up. At the higher firing rates (up to 6,000 RPM), the bursts are so short that the barrels can't heat up to the point of inducing damage. One should note that the barrels are also exposed to a constant stream of cooling air. In aircraft applications, the barrels are in a cool airstream. In all cases, the barrels spin as the gun fires, further increasing airflow and resulting in cooling.

The Drive Unit

The Vulcan's drive unit is located on the lower right rear of the rotor housing (as viewed from the front of the weapon). The very first Vulcan was electrically driven, and many current applications of the weapon are powered by an electric motor. In other aircraft applications, drive power is provided by the aircraft hydraulic system. Some variants even use engine-bled air to power the Vulcan drive unit. One particularly interesting application is the SUU-23/A gun pod, which contains a 20mm Vulcan and is mounted on the aircraft's exterior (typically under the wing or on a center station, like a bomb). The SUU-23/A uses the Gatling's own gas (i.e., the gas generated by the firing rounds) to drive the gun. The gun requires an input to initiate firing, but once the system is moving, it is essentially self-propelled. (More information on the SUU-23/A gun pod is included in Chapter 14.)

Firing rates on Vulcans range up to 6,000 RPM (the Vulcan can actually fire at 7,200 shots per minute, but this rate is unnecessarily high and imposes undue loads on the gun). Most applications utilize two selectable speeds. Aircraft typically have systems that can be fired at 4,000 or 6,000 RPM. The Vulcan Air Defense System can be fired at 1,000 or 3,000 RPM. Other systems fire at different rates, depending on the application and intended targets.

The Feeder and Ammunition Handling System

The Gatling gun feed and ammunition handling system was one of Dr. Gatling's greatest design challenges. Even on modern Gatling guns, the feed system is generally one of the most complicated mechanisms. Today's Gatlings use a feeder (typically located on the right side of the rotor housing) to accept each round from the ammunition chuting and place it into the rotor in front of each barrel's bolt. The feeder is gear-driven by the rotor. Once again, the guide bar located on the rotor housing's interior forces each spent cartridge out of the rotor and places it in exit chuting to either be returned to a storage area or dumped overboard.

The ammunition handling systems of modern Gatling guns represent significant mechanical engineering accomplishments. They rapidly transport large quantities of ammunition, provide a storage container for the ammunition, and in most cases, chuting to deliver the rounds to the gun's feeder.

Some feed systems are quite simple. The towed Vulcan Air Defense System, for example, simply hangs linked 20mm ammunition in a rectangular box on the right side of the gun. As the gun fires, the linked ammunition is pulled into it, the links are stripped off, the rounds are fired, and the empty cartridges are dumped overboard.

Other systems have complex helical storage drums, with chutes that basically have carriers for each round (this concept is explained in more detail in Chapter 11, which discusses the A-10's GAU-8/A gun system). On many aircraft, similar chuting returns the spent cartridges to the rear of the storage drum (taking the place of those already on their way to be fired) in lieu of allowing them to fall into the airstream. The reason for this is that it would be undesirable to have cartridge cases entering the airstream, where they might strike other friendly aircraft or perhaps be sucked into an engine inlet.

The mechanical strains on Vulcan ammunition handling systems are extreme (the 20mm rounds are being fed into the gun at rates as high as 6,000 RPM). When the ammunition feed requirement is coupled with other typical aircraft requirements to minimize weight, interesting mechanical concepts emerge.

An entire industry has grown up around the feed systems for modern Gatlings. In addition to General Electric, other companies design and produce loading and feed systems for these weapons as well. One of these is Western Design in California, a company that produces a unique linear linkless feed system. The advantage of this system is that it uses a rectilinear ammunition storage container (other systems typically store ammunition in right circular cylinders). Western Design's linear linkless feed systems can minimize volumetric requirements in certain applications, which is highly desirable in many of today's complex aircraft and other weapons platforms.

The Recoil Adaptors

The Vulcan cannon has three mounting points: a ball joint at the rear of the rotor housing and two recoil adaptors located on either side of the front of the rotor housing. The recoil adaptors are essentially shock absorbers that minimize the cyclic recoil impulses from the gun system. These forces can be significant. When firing at the maximum rate of 6,000 RPM, the 20mm Vulcan generates nearly 4,000 pounds of recoil force!

From Yesterday to Today

Modern Gatling guns, as represented by the 20mm Vulcan, have been upgraded from the early Gatlings in terms of ballistic performance, drive power, fire control, metallurgy, and a host of other factors. The improvements and capabilities of the 20mm are impressive, but the gun's similarity to its predecessors in terms of design features, principle of operation, and weapon systems applications is perhaps even more amazing. Keep these similarities in mind as you read the remaining chapters on current and future applications of the Gatling gun.

CHAPTER 9

Gatling Guns
Take to the Air

The Israeli F-15 pilot watched the screen in front of him as well as the skies outside the canopy. He was over the Bekaa Valley, and, in addition to the deadly SAM sites, he knew from the intelligence briefings that Syrian MiGs were in the area. He faced two threats, both deadly, and both providing but a second or two of reaction time.

Suddenly, his helmet-mounted speakers emitted a faint signal. He looked at his instruments, which said the same thing. Something out there had a lock on the F-15.

The pilot rolled the big F-15 sharply to the right and pulled the throttles rearward, winding down the nearly 50,000 pounds of Pratt and Whitney thrust. It worked. The Syrian MiG shot in front of him, perhaps a mile off to the left.

The Israeli locked on to the MiG with one of his Sidewinders, but before he realized what happened, the MiG pulled the same tactic on him. The Israeli didn't overshoot (he kept the MiG in front of the F-15), but he was now too close to fire the Sidewinder.

The Syrian pilot began rocking his MiG violently back and forth, knowing the F-15 was on his tail, and knowing that he couldn't out-zoom the American-built aircraft.

The Israeli knew his target was within the F-15's gun envelope. He flipped the joystick-mounted arm/safe switch to the armed position. He waited to watch the MiG's motions for another two seconds and realized the pilot's attempts at evasion were predictable rolls to the left and right. The Israeli fired a short burst (at the Gatling's lower speed of 4,000 RPM) slightly to the right of the MiG, anticipating that it would roll into the burst. The Syrian aircraft couldn't have been more than 300 meters in front of him.

The Israeli pilot had guessed correctly. The MiG's right wing disintegrated and fell away rapidly. The Israeli didn't look for a chute, nor did he divert course. He had ordnance to deliver, and he recognized that the MiG was but a minor disturbance to his mission.

As development of the M61 cannon neared completion in the mid-1950s (refer to Chapter 7), a question naturally arose as to which aircraft would mount the new gun system first. Several new jets (the "Century-series," so called because of the numerical designations) were in development during this era. These included the North American F-100 Super Sabre (first flown in May 1953), the McDonnell Douglas F-101 Voodoo (first flown in September 1954), the Convair F-102 Delta Dagger (first flown in October 1953), the Lockheed F-104 Starfighter (first flown in March 1954), the Fairchild Republic F-105 Thunderchief (first flown in October 1955), and the General Dynamics F-106 Delta Dart (first flown in December 1956).

Each of these aircraft had distinct missions, which—when coupled with the arguments concerning the efficiency of guns versus missiles for air combat—influenced their selection of armament. The F-100 was intended to be a supersonic air superiority fighter. The F-101 was developed to meet the need for long-range fighter escort services, primarily for the new strategic air command. The F-102 originated as a result of the need for a long-range interceptor capable of bringing down manned Soviet bombers. The F-104 was a return to the requirement for an air superiority fighter (it was to be a small, light, and highly maneuverable aircraft, strongly influenced by the air combat experienced during the Korean conflict). The F-105 was designed as a high-performance fighter bomber, with an internal weapons bay capable of carrying nuclear munitions. Finally, the F-106 was an outgrowth of the F-102 program, but with more stringent interception requirements.

Guns Versus Missiles

The debate concerning the relative merits of guns versus missiles for air-to-air combat is one that has arisen frequently throughout the post-World War II history of aviation development. It first emerged during the Century-series developmental phase (and continues to this day as the United States ponders the requirements for the Advanced Tactical Fighter and other advanced aircraft).

The guns-versus-missiles argument is centered primarily on whether air-to-air combat will be fought at very short ranges (i.e., those ranges within which aircraft can engage other aircraft with guns) or at distances exceeding gun ranges (typically more than a kilometer or so).

To better understand the argument, one must know the relative merits of each in air-to-air combat. The chief advantages of a missile as an air-to-air weapon are its guidance and range capabilities. Unlike cannon fire, which simply follows a ballistic trajectory, missiles typically have sophisticated infrared-seeking capabilities and/or radar guidance. These guidance systems assure a very high kill probability.

On that basis, many argued fervently for the outright elimination of gun systems on modern tactical aircraft, reasoning that air-to-air missiles (particularly when coupled with on-board radar systems) would enable pilots to defeat enemy air combat fighters at extended ranges. To a great extent, such logic was sound. During the 1950s, the United States had developed an extremely capable air-to-air missile (the Sidewinder), which even today remains a frontline, state-of-the-art weapon. Most U.S. air-to-air combat victories in Vietnam were attained with the Sidewinder.

Unfortunately, these same capabilities lend themselves to the missile's chief disadvantages, including the high costs associated with guidance and propulsion systems and the potentially low reliability that results from the complexities associated with such systems.

Another set of disadvantages associated with missiles is the minimum range requirement. An aircraft cannot engage another at extremely close range with missiles. If an enemy air combat fighter manages to maneuver into close range, an aircraft armed solely with missiles is essentially defenseless. A related disadvantage is the relatively long time it takes to achieve target lock-on. This time, which can be as much as a few seconds, could conceivably provide a gun-armed enemy aircraft the slight margin required for victory (by allowing maneuvering to within less than the missiles' minimum engagement ring).

Based on all of the above, the bottom line during the 1950s was that most defense department planners were convinced that the air-to-

Figure 16. The M61A1 Vulcan cannon. This modern 20mm Gatling gun, designed and manufactured by General Electric, is standard armament for many modern tactical fighters. This is the F-18 Hornet application, including the cannon, its ammunition storage drum, and the chuting to carry live rounds to the gun and fired cases back to the drum. Different aircraft have different gun and storage drum layouts due to space and aircraft configuration considerations.

67

air missile had irrevocably altered the course of future air combat. Consequently, guns were not considered essential elements of all new fighter aircraft armament suites. Nonetheless, the 20mm M61 Vulcan gun was incorporated into the Lockheed F-104 Starfighter, the Fairchild Republic F-105 Thunderchief, and the General Dynamics F-106 Delta Dart fuselage designs. The F-104 was the first production fighter to fly with the Vulcan cannon.

The F-4 Phantom Development Program

The F-4 Phantom also entered development during the 1950s. This is significant in that it demonstrates the continuing re-emergence of the guns-versus-missiles argument. Also, no discussion of U.S. fighter aircraft can be considered complete without mention of the F-4. McDonnell Douglas and others (under license) have manufactured variants of the F-4 for more than twenty years, delivering more than five thousand of these awesome fighters. The F-4 has been a frontline fighter for the U.S. Air Force, Navy, and Marine Corps (and the air forces of numerous U.S. allies) for three decades.

When the F-4 entered development in the 1950s the armament concept included four single-barreled 20mm guns, but these were subsequently dropped in favor of missiles as the aircraft's mission changed to that of an all-weather interceptor. It wasn't until the fifth variant of the F-4 emerged (the F-4E, fielded in 1967 as a response to the requirements of the Vietnam War) that an internally mounted 20mm Vulcan was included. Today, however, almost any version of the F-4 can carry the 20mm Vulcan Gatling gun in an externally mounted centerline pod. The aircraft can also carry a similar pod-mounted 30mm Gatling. (More information on these pod-mounted guns is included in Chapter 14.)

Gatlings on Bombers

For a brief period, strategic bombing mission scenarios mandated the inclusion of guns on bombers for defense against enemy interceptors. Accordingly, the ill-fated B-58 Hustler flew with a 20mm Vulcan. The B-58 was a 1950s-era nuclear bomber, but the plane was a maintenance nightmare and was soon dropped from the active inventory. The Boeing B-52 Stratofortress was much more successful. It began development in 1948, first flew in 1952, and has continued as a U.S. Air Force frontline strategic and tactical bomber for nearly forty years. Even though newer strategic bombers have emerged (e.g., the F-111, the B-1, and the B-2 Stealth Bomber), the B-52 will likely remain in service past the turn of the century. The latest version of the B-52 (the B-52H) has a single 20mm Vulcan mounted in its tail. Initially, B-52s were equipped with four .50-caliber Browning machine guns, but when the last variant of the B-52 (the H model) was fielded in 1960, the smaller .50-caliber weapons were replaced with the M61 Vulcan. The concept was to provide effective defense against enemy interceptors. B-52s saw extensive use in Vietnam as tactical bombers, and there are at least two instances of B-52s shooting down MiGs in that conflict with their Gatlings.

The General Dynamics F-111 is another aircraft with a controversial background. Even though the F-111 carries the designation of a fighter, it is a bomber in reality. Like the B-52H, it also carries an internally mounted 20mm M61 Vulcan. The F-111 was developed in the early 1960s and was intended to be a "do-everything" aircraft. It was envisioned as both a fighter and a bomber. Secretary of Defense Robert McNamara even pushed it as a carrier-based aircraft (the U.S. Navy never adopted the F-111 or any of its variants, however).

The multirole controversy was further compounded by the rush to put the F-111 into service during the Vietnam conflict (the aircraft's first flight was in 1967, and it was sent to Vietnam shortly thereafter). Several aircraft were mysteriously lost in combat, which was later discovered to be the result of poor-quality welding in the F-111's tail-control actuation mechanism. Other problems that plagued the aircraft included its controversial swing-wing design (and the tendency of the wing hinge to develop cracks), and the program's enormous cost overruns (which reduced initial procurement to just over one-third of the planned 210 aircraft).

The air force ultimately came to the realization that the F-111 was not really a fighter at all, but a superb bomber. In fact, for a period it was the air force's only all-weather, day-or-night, pinpoint-accuracy bomber. The United States maintains F-111 bomber squadrons in England (these were used in the mid-1980s strike against Libya) and in the continental United States. The Royal Australian Air Force is also equipped with the F-111.

Gatlings on Fighters

In addition to the fighter aircraft already mentioned, one should recognize that nearly every contemporary American air combat fighter and many attack aircraft fly with a variant of the Gatling gun. There are a few exceptions (mostly aircraft that carry multiple .50-caliber, 20mm, or 30mm single-barreled cannon, such as F-5, the A-4, and the F-8). Almost any fighter or attack aircraft, however, can be configured to carry pod-mounted Gatlings.

The subject of pod-mounted Gatlings is somewhat difficult to treat accurately because of the infinite variations possible, the large number of variants of particular aircraft models, and the numerous improvised configurations developed during the Vietnam conflict. However, non-pod-mounted Gatling applications for fixed-wing aircraft are summarized in Table 9-1.

The Gatling
Gun: 19th
Century
Machine Gun
to 21st
Century
Vulcan

70

Table 9-1
Gatling Gun Fixed Wing Aircraft Applications

Aircraft	Manufacturer	Gatling Type	Caliber	Mounting
AC-47	Douglas	3 GAU-2B/As	7.62mm	fuselage
AC-119G	Fairchild	4MXU-470s	7.62mm	fuselage
AC-119K	Fairchild	4 MXU-470s, 2 M61s	7.62mm and 20mm	fuselage
AC-130A	Lockheed	4 MXU-470s, 4 M61s	7.62mm and 20mm	fuselage
AC-130E	Lockheed	2 MXU-470s, 2 M61s	7.62mm and 20mm	fuselage
AC-130H	Lockheed	2 MXU-470s, 2 M61s	7.62mm and 20mm	fuselage
AV-8	McDonnell Douglas	GAU-12/A	25mm	fuselage
A-10	Fairchild	GAU-8/A	30mm	fuselage
A-37	Cessna	GAU-2B/A	7.62mm	nose
A-7	Vought	M61	20mm	fuselage
B-52	Boeing	M61	20mm	tail
B-58	General Dynamics	M61	20mm	tail
F-104	Lockheed	M61	20mm	fuselage
F-105	Republic	M61	20mm	fuselage
F-106	General Dynamics	M61	20mm	fuselage
F-111	General Dynamics	M61	20mm	fuselage
F-14	Grumman	M61	20mm	fuselage
F-15	McDonnell Douglas	M61	20mm	rt strake
F-16	General Dynamics	M61	20mm	lt strake
F-18	McDonnell Douglas	M61	20mm	fuselage
F-4	McDonnell Douglas	M61	20mm	fuselage
OV-10	Rockwell	M197	20mm	fuselage
S-2	Grumman	GAU-2B/A	7.62mm	fuselage

An Antitank Gatling

Another highly unusual Gatling application occurs in the Fairchild A-10 Thunderbolt, which carries the most powerful Gatling ever built. The A-10's 30mm Gatling gun was designed specifically to defeat Soviet tanks, and the A-10 was the first aircraft to be designed around a Gatling gun. (The A-10 and its 30mm GAU-8/A Gatling cannon are described in detail in Chapter 11.)

Gatlings on Gunships

One of the most interesting of all Gatling applications is the U.S. Air Force gunship story, which involves the placement of numerous Gatlings on highly modified propeller-driven cargo aircraft. These became some of the most heavily armed aircraft in aviation history, and they have been used in a variety of combat roles in Southeast Asia, Grenada, Panama, the Middle East, and probably various classified

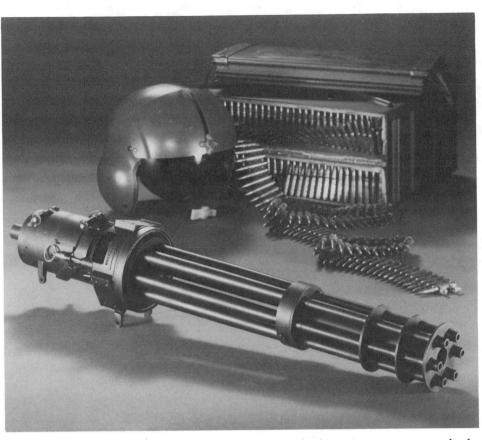

operations. (Chapter 10 will discuss these specialized aircraft in greater detail.)

Gatlings on Helicopters

The helicopter saw limited use as a combat vehicle in the Korean conflict and then extensive use in Vietnam. As the helicopter was recognized as a stable gun platform ideally suited for air-to-ground attack and air-support, the Gatling gun quite naturally found its way into several such applications.

The initial application of guns to helicopters occurred during the Korean War. Typically, this consisted of .30-caliber Browning machine guns on pintle mounts in the helicopters' doors. Door-mounted helicopter guns were used in a ground suppression fire support role to a much larger extent in Vietnam. Typically 7.62mm M60 light machine guns in the doors of Huey helicopters, these were only moderately effective and quite inaccurate.

In addition to the door mounts, a variety of special turrets were developed. These typically were mounted on the side of the helicopter or, more commonly, underneath the fuselage. Some had aiming systems linked to the gunner's line of sight, such that the gun was always aimed at whatever the pilot viewed.

Helicopter armament came of age during the U.S. involvement in Vietnam. New helicopter assault tactics were developed, and with them came new applications of the Gatling gun, new Gatling guns, and even new helicopters. One example was the placement of the 5.56mm XM214 Gatling on the Huey (this gun fired the same round as the M16 infantry rifle). The XM214 five-barreled Gatling gun could fire at up to 10,000 RPM. Another was the GAU-2B/A 7.62mm Gatling, which also found a home on the Huey. Yet another was the 12.7mm (the old .50-caliber Browning machine gun round) Gatling, in both three- and six-barreled versions. The .50-caliber Gatling gun (known as the GECAL

Figure 17. The 7.62mm mini-gun. This six-barreled .30-caliber weapon fires the NATO standard 7.62mm round. It has found a home on a variety of rotary and fixed-wing aircraft.

The Gatling
Gun: 19th
Century
Machine Gun
to 21st
Century
Vulcan

72

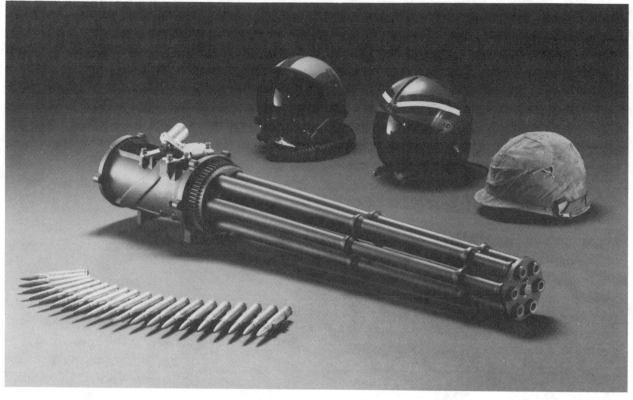

50, and shown in Figure 18) was an outgrowth of the Grenada incursion, in which the 7.62mm was found to be only marginally effective against hardened targets. The GECAL 50 is mounted on the army's new Blackhawk helicopter. It will also find a home on the developmental V-22 Osprey, a vertical takeoff and landing aircraft.

The Huey Cobra was developed by Bell Helicopter during the Vietnam conflict. It was initially intended to be an interim weapons platform until the army fielded its planned Apache attack helicopter, but the Cobra took on a life of its own. It became the first armed helicopter developed exclusively as such.

The Cobra can carry an impressive array of weapons, including several antitank missiles, rockets, and a variety of gun systems. Several Gatling gun variants have been fitted to the Cobra, including the basic 7.62mm version, a turret with either two 7.62mm Gatlings or one Gatling and a 40mm grenade launcher, the M197 three-barreled 20mm Gatling, and the GAU-12/U five-barreled 25mm Gatling. Different weapons have been fitted in accordance with customer specifications. The Cobra is currently flying with the U.S. Army, the U.S. Marine Corps, and the armed forces of Israel, Jordan, Pakistan, and Japan.

When the Apache attack helicopter finally materialized in 1982 (the Cobra had been an "interim" attack helicopter since 1965), it included a 30mm Hughes Chain Gun in its nose turret instead of a Gatling. The Chain Gun is a single-barreled weapon that uses a chain

Figure 18. General Electric's GECAL 50 .50-caliber Gatling gun. Both three- and six-barreled versions of this weapon are offered, with firing rates up to 10,000 RPM.

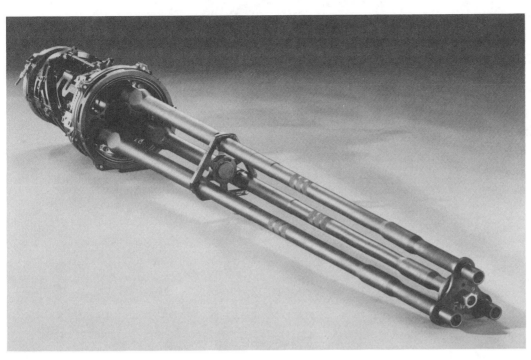

drive to cycle the action.

One other most unusual aircraft that bears further mention is the Bell/Boeing V-22 Osprey, which is being developed for the U.S. Marine Corps. The V-22 is a tilt-wing aircraft. It can tilt its engines straight up (thereby pointing its over-sized twin propellers upward) and take off, land, and hover like a helicopter. The V-22 can also bring its engines and propellers forward and fly like a conventional fixed-wing aircraft. As is the case with any new aircraft, the V-22 is experiencing a turbulent development program. The aircraft appears to be technically sound, but congressional and service support (and therefore funding levels) have varied. The aircraft is mentioned here because its planned armament also includes the 25mm GAU-12/U Gatling (in addition to the GECAL 50, as mentioned earlier).

In addition to those mentioned above, a variety of other helicopters have been armed with Gatling guns. Table 9-2 summarizes Gatling-armed rotary-wing aircraft.

Figure 19. The M197 Vulcan cannon. This 20mm Gatling, a three-barreled version of the M61A1 Vulcan, has been fitted to several aircraft.

Table 9-2
Gatling Gun Rotary Wing Applications

Aircraft	Manufacturer	Gatling Type	Caliber
AH-1 Cobra	Bell	M197	20mm
AH-1 Cobra	Bell	GAU-12/U	25mm
AH-1 Cobra	Bell	M28	7.62mm
CH-47 Chinook	Bell	SUU-11B/A	7.62mm
CH-53 Super Jolly	Sikorsky	M134	7.62mm
H-2 Seasprite	Kaman	M134	7.62mm
H-76 Eagle	Sikorsky	M134	7.62mm
OH-58 Kiowa	Bell	M134	7.62mm

Aircraft	Manufacturer	Gatling Type	Caliber
OH-6 Cayuse	McDonnell Douglas	M134	7.62mm
UH-1 Huey	Bell	M134	7.62mm
UH-1 Huey	Bell	GECAL 50	12.7mm
UH-1 Huey	Bell	XM214	5.56mm
UH-60 Black Hawk	Sikorsky	M134	7.62mm
UH-60 Black Hawk	Sikorsky	GECAL 50	12.7mm
V-22 Osprey	Bell	GAU-12/U	25mm

The Gatling
Gun: 19th
Century
Machine Gun
to 21st
Century
Vulcan

74

10 The Gunship Story

*T*he roar from the twin rotary-pistoned engines was nearly deafening as the lumbering AC-47 circled the overrun Special Forces base camp high in the Laotian mountains. The aircrew regarded the noise as a nuisance, but to the Green Beret colonel and the six surviving NCOs in the command bunker in the center of the overrun camp, it sounded wonderful.

"Sierra Foxtrot Seven, this is Puff, over," the colonel heard on his portable radio. Three shots rang out from an NCO's M16 as he killed a North Vietnamese regular who tried to penetrate the bunker. The colonel looked up to see if the sergeant would fire any more, and when it appeared that he wouldn't, the colonel keyed the microphone and spoke.

"Roger, Puff, we hear you. Request saturation fire over our camp, over," the colonel said.

"Sierra Fox, aren't your people in the camp? Over," the aircraft commander responded.

"We're under sandbags in the center," the colonel said. "Any of ours out there are already dead, over."

"Roger, Sierra Fox. Out," the pilot answered. The AC-47 pulled into a tighter orbit over the base camp. Some of the North Vietnamese fired futilely at the old Douglas aircraft with their AK-47s, but none of their bullets connected. The pilot entered what was to become a classic gunship pylon orbit, and the gunners opened fire. The AC-47s three miniguns rained .30-caliber projectiles on the target at a rate of 18,000 RPM. The earth jumped into the air as the bullets impacted only inches apart throughout the interior of the camp's perimeter. All of the North Vietnamese soldiers lay lifeless, their bodies twitching only when struck by the 147-grain full-metal-jacket projectiles.

During the early stages of the Vietnam War, the U.S. Air Force recognized the need for an aircraft that could fly at low altitudes, remain aloft for long periods of time, and place saturation fire on lightly armored targets. To meet this need, vintage World War II Douglas C-47 cargo planes were pulled from storage and equipped with side-mounted 7.62mm Gatling-based Vulcans. The new AC-47s were enormously successful. But actually, the concept of the side-firing airborne weapons platform preceded the Vietnam War by several decades.

The Early Days

The concept of the side-firing weapons platform emerged in 1926, when 1st Lt. Fred Nelson of the U.S. Army mounted a .30-caliber machine gun on the side of a de Havilland DH-4 biplane. Nelson's idea was that if he flew a low-altitude, banked turn around an imaginary point on the ground (a pylon turn), the side-mounted machine gun would remain aimed at the target during the maneuver. The test may have been successful (no records were kept), but as the United States was not at war, there was no need to take the concept further.

The idea reemerged in 1945, when a gentleman named Gilmore MacDonald suggested that it could be used for air attack of surfaced enemy submarines. He even went so far as to suggest the use of an aircraft armed with a bazooka, reasoning that its armor-penetrating capabilities would be more effective than machine gun fire. MacDonald's idea died in 1945 for the same reason that Nelson's did in 1926. World War II ended, and the need for such a weapon disappeared.

MacDonald was convinced that the side-firing airborne weapons platform was a sound concept, though, and he resubmitted the idea to the U.S. Air Force Tactical Air Command in September 1961. The air force turned it down again, but shortly thereafter a fortuitous event occurred. While on reserve duty at Eglin Air Force Base, MacDonald met Ralph Flexman, a Bell Aero Systems engineer. The two men refined the concept, and Flexman submitted it to the U.S. Air Force Systems Command in December 1962. In his letter to the air force, Flexman explained the theoretical advantages of a side-firing weapons platform: ". . . lateral firing, while making a pylon turn, will prove effective in controlling ground fire . . ."

Around this time the Vietnam War was beginning to intensify, and Flexman's letter reached the right people. In May 1962, the systems command at Wright-Patterson Air Force Base initiated a low-key effort known as Project Tailchase. The project involved flying the types of maneuvers Flexman proposed in an old T-28 test aircraft. The T-28, flown by Capt. John Simons, used a rather unsophisticated grease pencil line as a sighting device to determine whether a constant aim point could be maintained. The tests were strictly for sighting; no armament of any type was used. Simons' initial tests were successful, and the concept began to gain momentum. In January 1963, Simons flew a C-131 cargo plane equipped with special cameras to further develop lateral sighting techniques. These tests continued into 1964, all without any live firing. In mid-1964 the Aeronautical Systems

Division at Wright-Patterson Air Force Base was searching for new weapon employment ideas to meet deficiencies in existing tactical capabilities. Capt. Ron Terry, a Vietnam veteran who was part of the team assigned to this search, reviewed the files on Project Tailchase and recognized the capabilities it suggested.

The next step was a live-fire test. The Aeronautical Systems Division's Limited Warfare Office and the Flight Test Operations group at Wright-Patterson developed a test program that utilized a 7.62mm Gatling-type mini-gun mounted in a C-131. The tests, flown at Eglin Air Force Base in August of 1964, were extremely successful. The feasibility of the concept and the deepening involvement in Vietnam led to the AC-47 Dragon Ship program.

The AC-47 Dragon Ship

The need for an airborne platform capable of delivering saturation fire had become so great that the gunship program proceeded at great speed. In September of 1964, only one month after the first live-fire test, three MXU-470/A 7.62mm mini-guns were mounted to fire out the left side of an old Douglas C-47. This aircraft was tested at Eglin, and in December Captain Terry took it to Vietnam.

The new gunship was designated the AC-47 Dragon Ship and assigned to the 1st Air Commando Squadron. Captain Terry and his crew were assigned to roving patrol missions and soon showed the AC-47 to be quite effective. Several more AC-47s were built by E-Systems in Greenville, Texas, and sent to Vietnam. The AC-47s worked primarily at night to defend Special Forces base camps and air base perimeters, using their sensors and illuminators to find targets of opportunity.

Captured enemy soldiers admitted they were terrified of the AC-47. Capable of firing all three guns at a combined rate of 18,000 RPM, the AC-47 was described by the Vietcong as a "fire-breathing dragon." The description took, and the aircraft became known as "Puff, the Magic Dragon." Later on, it became known as "Spooky," no doubt to describe the effect it created when firing.

There were problems with the AC-47, though. The basic aircraft, having first flown in 1935, was generally acknowledged to be underpowered and overburdened. Another detraction was the limited effective range of the 7.62mm mini-guns. This required the AC-47 to fly at relatively low altitudes, making it extremely vulnerable to antiaircraft fire. In certain operational scenarios, however, the AC-47 was an ideal aircraft for the ground saturation-fire mission (as demonstrated by the fact that, even today, the Salvadoran Air Force is considering modifying as many as five C-47s to the AC-47 configuration). The United States recognized that requirements for new mission capabilities were developing in Vietnam, though. Existing AC-47s were transferred to the South Vietnamese air force, and work began on an even more powerful gunship.

The AC-130 Spectre

In an effort to address some of the AC-47's deficiencies, the air force began to develop a highly modified version of the C-130 Lockheed "Hercules." During all of the AC-47 development work and combat deployments, Captain Terry was formulating an idea for an even more powerful weapons platform. He presented his concept to senior air force officers, and they approved it. The Aeronautical Systems Division at Wright-Patterson Air Force Base supplied a C-130A cargo plane, which was—and still is—the largest propeller-driven cargo aircraft in the air force inventory.

E-Systems of Dallas, Texas, mounted four 7.62mm mini-guns and four 20mm Vulcans in the C-130A. As had been the case on the earlier gunships, all were mounted to fire out the left side of the aircraft. Live firing tests of the new AC-130A were conducted at Eglin Air Force Base in June 1967.

Interestingly, the test that had the most influence on the decision to continue the AC-130 gunship project actually represented a significant failure. In this test, the first AC-130A was supposed to fire a 5-second burst from all eight Gatling guns as the aircraft executed a pylon turn. Several high-level air force dignitaries witnessed the test, but what they saw was a far cry from a short 5-second burst. An electron-

Figure 20. An AC-130 Spectre over Hurlburt Field, Florida. These aircraft, which flew successfully in Vietnam and several other U.S. military actions (including Grenada and Panama), are normally based out of Duke Field on the Gulf of Mexico. The aircraft is simulating the banked pylon turn it would fly when engaging a target. The pods on the left side include a laser and other target-sensing and ranging devices.

ics failure in the gunfire control circuitry caused all eight guns to continue firing after the trigger had been released. The pilot kept the AC-130A in its pylon turn until all eight guns ran out of ammunition, which lasted for about one orbit of the aircraft. The effect was spectacular. All eight guns were firing tracer ammunition—the 7.62mm Gatlings at 6,000 RPM and the 20mm Gatlings at 2,500 RPM. The AC-130A was delivering a concentrated spray of tracer ammunition at a combined rate of 34,000 RPM!

The generals and other dignitaries witnessing the test did not know there had been a failure. They thought the massive display of lethality had been planned. They were most impressed, particularly in light of the perimeter defense and Ho Chi Minh Trail problems being experienced in Southeast Asia. Shortly thereafter, Captain Terry was given permission to take his AC-130A to Vietnam. He returned to Vietnam with the AC-130A in September 1967 and became Detachment 2 of the 14th Air Commando Wing. The new AC-130A was nicknamed "Superspook" in direct reference to its AC-47 heritage. The name was later changed to Spectre.

Soon after arriving in Vietnam, Captain Terry was promoted to major, and a second AC-130A arrived in Vietnam. This aircraft kept the four 7.62mm mini-guns and two of the 20mm Vulcans, but it replaced the other two Vulcans with two 40mm Bofors automatic cannons. The Bofors is a single-barreled gun system capable of firing 125 shots per minute (it is not based on the Gatling principle). The new AC-130A also had a more advanced fire-control system. As had been the case on all AC-series gunships, all weapons fired from the left side of the aircraft.

Major Terry's two AC-130As became legendary in Vietnam, rapidly earning the aircraft a reputation as a most valuable interdiction weapon.

Figure 21 "From Spooky to Spectre," an air force painting showing both the AC-47 and AC-130 gunships engaging targets.

The Spectre soon acquired yet another nickname, "Truckbuster," because of the incredible lethality the two aircraft displayed in stopping traffic along the Ho Chi Minh Trail. In less than three years, the two AC-130As destroyed more than five thousand enemy trucks.

The AC-119 Shadow and Stinger

The AC-130 was enormously effective in Vietnam, but there simply weren't enough of the big gunships to meet the demands for their services. In an effort to address this deficiency, the air force began work on a modified Fairchild C-119 "Flying Boxcar," the twin-boom cargo plane developed and fielded in the closing days of World War II. The original version of the C-119-based gunship was the AC-119G, nicknamed the "Stinger," which first flew in 1967.

The Stinger's two 3,350-horsepower Wright radial piston engines gave it more power than the AC-47. It had four 7.62mm mini-guns, all firing out the left side. Other equipment included a night illumination system, image intensifiers, a fire-control computer, various optical sighting systems, a flare launcher, and crew armor protection. In all, twenty-six AC-119Gs were built.

Even with its enhanced target acquisition capabilities and additional firepower, though, the AC-119G still suffered from the same problems as the AC-47. With all of the added equipment the AC-119G was carrying, it was overburdened. Also, it did not offer any increase in maximum effective range for its primary armament. Even though it added a fourth mini-gun, that was only 7.62mm. The AC-119G could put more firepower on the target, but it still had to get fairly close to the target to do so.

To solve these problems, the air force next fielded the AC-119K, nicknamed the "Shadow." The AC-119K offered significant improvements in armament and propulsion. It kept the four 7.62mm mini-guns of the AC-119G and added two 20mm Vulcans. The 20mm Vulcans gave the SAC-119K significantly greater standoff from the target, and for the first time, the capability of delivering high-explosive projectiles. Like its predecessors, the AC-119K also represented the largest concentration of airborne Gatling-based firepower ever flown. All six weapons fired from the left side of the aircraft, and the basic ammunition load exceeded 100,000 rounds. To overcome the power problems suffered by both the AC-47 and the AC-119G, the AC-119K was equipped with two General Electric 2,850-pound thrust turbojets mounted in pods underneath the wings. The jet engines augmented the older radial piston engines so that the AC-119K was both propeller- and jet-driven.

The Shadow also offered several improvements in terms of target-acquisition capability. In addition to the equipment carried by the AC-119G, the AC-119K had a forward-looking infrared sensor, a forward- and side-looking radar, and precision navigation and communication equipment.

There were twenty-six AC-119K Shadows built for a total of fifty-two AC-119 gunships. These aircraft were later retired as the Vietnam War wound down and more AC-130 gunships were added to the inventory.

Tactics

As of this writing, all of the U.S. AC-47s and AC-119s are retired. The U.S. Air Force relies heavily on the AC-130, however, for a variety of military operations. The AC-130 series of gunships usually carries a crew of fourteen airmen and officers. The crew includes a pilot, a copilot, a navigator, a flight engineer, a fire-control officer, an electronic warfare officer, two sensor operators, one illuminator operator, and five gunners. The aircraft mission includes close air support, armed interdiction, reconnaissance, armed escort, forward control, and search and rescue.

As mentioned earlier, the AC-130 earned its "truckbusting" reputation primarily on the basis of its armed interdiction mission on the Ho Chi Minh Trail. An engagement normally began with one of the sensor operators acquiring a target, which was usually a column of trucks.

The AC-130A is equipped with low-light-level television (capable of collecting and displaying images in low-light conditions), forward-looking infrared, radar, and optical sensors. Once the target is spotted, it is handed off to the pilot and the illuminator operator. The pilot has a gunsight with two pips (or dots) displayed on a screen. One pip represents the target, and the other represents the predicted gunfire impact point. The illuminator operator (sometimes referred to as the "vertical observer" because of the manner in which he hangs out of the rear of the aircraft) assists the pilot by training the 2,000-watt illuminator on the target, and by releasing flares for the same purpose. The illuminator operator also gives the pilot information on how to position and maneuver the aircraft. The pilot adjusts the angle of bank, speed, and altitude until the two gunsight pips are superimposed. At this point, the gunners fire at the target. The illuminator operator spots where the gunfire impacts and provides feedback to the pilot and crew to adjust fire as necessary.

Normally, the tactic employed when engaging a column of enemy trucks along the Ho Chi Minh Trail was to engage the first and last trucks in the column, thereby anchoring the column in place. The AC-130A would then continue to orbit, destroying the entire column.

AC-130A Enhancements

Major Terry continued to push for even more powerful versions of the AC-130A, and in February 1972, his efforts resulted in the AC-130E. The AC-130E gunship had four 7.62mm mini-guns, two 20mm Vulcans, one 40mm Bofors automatic cannon, and (incredibly) a direct-fire 105mm howitzer. A little more than a year later, the AC-130F was redesignated the AC-130H. The AC-130H incorporated a laser target designator and in-flight refueling capability. This aircraft could also be optionally armed with bomblet dispensers, grenade projectors, and rocket pods.

Gunships Today

Today, both the AC-130A and the AC-130H fly with the U.S. Air Force. The 919th Special Operations Group, an Air Force Reserve unit based at Duke Field in Florida, flies ten AC-130As. This unit, which first received the AC-130 in June of 1975, is charged with the mission of providing "an operationally ready force capable of providing close air support, armed reconnaissance, armed interdiction and escort, plus forward air control and search and rescue missions in the AC-130A aircraft."

One of the more interesting applications of this mission occurs every time the space shuttle lifts off from Cape Kennedy. The 919th supports the lift-off with three AC-130As. The gunships use their forward-looking infrared and low-light-level television sensors to provide surveillance of the launch site and surrounding areas. They also keep the flight corridor from the launch site to the rocket motor splashdown area clear. The three AC-130As are also ready for search and rescue duty should a shuttle launch be aborted. On the very first shuttle launch, the 2000-watt illuminator was used to light the way for the astronauts when they traveled from the operations building to the shuttle.

The Tactical Air Command's Special Operations Wing at Hurlburt Field (also in Florida) flies the AC-130H. This unit is part of the active air force and, like its reserve counterpart, has ten of the gunships (for a total of twenty in the air force inventory).

AC-130 crew members speak of the aircraft and its capabilities in glowing terms. The AC-130 family of gunships offers more firepower than any other close-air-support aircraft, three to five times the loiter capability of fighters (especially at low altitudes), greater accuracy, and greater ability to engage the enemy with a variety of sophisticated sensors and up to seven people looking for targets.

Summary

As is the case for many aircraft flying with Gatling guns, the AC-47, AC-119, and AC-130 family of gunships is one of the most intriguing stories in aviation history. From the AC-47 (which is still flying in the air forces of other nations) to the ultralethal AC-130H, the airborne gunship concept has proven its merit. The operations of the air force's two AC-130 units are shrouded in secrecy, which suggests the gunships still see combat duty (AC-130s are rumored to have participated in the recent Grenada and Panama actions). The gunship story is yet another tribute to the Gatling gun, as these gunships form a vital component of the United States' tactical air warfare capability.

11 The A-10 Thunderbolt Story

*A*s the column of Soviet armored vehicles rolled across the open Eastern European plain, the lumbering sound of diesel engines and clanking treads drowned out all else. Russian infantrymen struggled to keep up, shouting to (but not hearing) each other.

Suddenly, a roar different than that emanating from the tanks engulfed everything. It sounded like a powerful internal combustion engine (perhaps that of a race car) running at full throttle. The infantrymen started dropping as the tanks slowed to a stop. From the rear of the column, and working toward the front at an incredible rate, the ground erupted all around in 10-meter-wide explosions. Three of the tanks burst into flames, one blowing its turret off the hull. Black smoke was everywhere.

An A-10 passed overhead, its 30mm Avenger gun continuing to roar, throwing out high-velocity depleted uranium penetrators and a 20-foot-long muzzle flash. The aircraft swung low as it passed the column. One of the infantrymen not killed in the first pass realized that the devilish craft was circling for another pass, and in addition to feeling raw terror, he suddenly felt very ill.

Of all the Gatling-gun-equipped aircraft flying today, one of the most intriguing is the A-10 Thunderbolt II. Nicknamed the "Warthog" by the crews who fly it, the A-10 is the first airplane designed from the ground up around a Gatling gun. It carries the most powerful Gatling gun ever built.

The Close Air Support Problem

The need for the Thunderbolt II and its very specialized mission was recognized during the conflicts in Korea and Vietnam. In these conflicts, U.S. aircraft were the best in the world for air-to-air combat. In the Korean War, these superb fighters included the F-86 Sabre, F-84 Thunderjet, F-80 Shooting Star, and F9F Panther. The F-4 Phantom, the F-111, the F-8, the A-7, and several others saw action in the Vietnam War. Vietnam-era tactical aircraft included such features as supersonic speeds, terrain-following radar, computer-assisted weapon delivery systems, and even such things as exotic as wings with adjustable sweep angles.

One problem with these aircraft, however, was that they were designed primarily for air-to-air combat. This made them less than ideal for close-air-support missions (which support ground troops by engaging enemy ground targets). Having been designed for air-to-air combat, they had to be fast and maneuverable, and capable of flying at high altitudes. This placed constraints on the amount and kinds of ordnance that could be carried. Their high speed also meant the air-

planes had a high stall speed, which detracted from accurately delivering ground fire. In the close-air-support role, where the pilot would be required to engage ground targets in close proximity to friendly troops, inaccurate delivery systems were unacceptable.

Most of the aircraft that flew in Vietnam were designed with late 1950s and early 1960s technology. During that era, vulnerability to small-arms ground fire was not recognized as a key design parameter. Unfortunately, this is precisely the environment in which close-air-support aircraft must operate. In the Vietnam War, more U.S. aircraft were downed by small-arms fire than by any other means. There is even a confirmed case of an F-4 Phantom being shot down by a single rifle bullet.

The most significant drawback of existing close-air-support aircraft (i.e., those used in the close-air-support role prior to the advent of the A-10) was that they were ineffective against tanks. With enemy armor being one of the main threats to NATO forces in the European theater, military planners recognized that an aircraft with new capabilities was required.

The A-X Requirements

The close-air-support deficiencies the United States had observed during the Korean and Vietnam conflicts defined the need for the A-X aircraft in the mid-1960s (A-X stands for "Attack Experimental"). The air force initially envisioned a turbo-prop aircraft. The idea was that a current-technology version of the World War II Thunderbolt would best satisfy the requirements (note that World War II vintage Thunderbolts were used in a close-air-support role in Vietnam).

The A-X specification was based primarily on deficiencies in existing aircraft. One of the requirements was an extremely accurate ordnance delivery system, because friendly ground troops could be within yards of the enemy. A high payload was also needed. As explained earlier, most existing tactical aircraft had been designed to maximize either maneuverability, speed, altitude, or some combination of these parameters. Payload had necessarily suffered.

The A-X aircraft also had to be able to remain in the air near the target for long periods of time, which is referred to as "loiter capability." Existing tactical aircraft had been designed to operate at high altitudes. When flying at the low altitudes associated with close-air-support missions, they consumed excessive amounts of fuel. This translated to short loiter capabilities, which detracted from the effectiveness of close-air-support missions.

The air force also stipulated that the new A-X aircraft needed to have good "survivability" characteristics, meaning it should be relatively invulnerable to small-arms fire from the ground. To ensure that the aircraft met this requirement, the air force specified armor protection, redundant flight-control systems, and fire-suppression equipment.

The Armor Threat

The main requirement for the A-X aircraft, however, was that it be able to contribute significantly to the NATO defense of Eastern Europe, and that meant it had to be able to defeat tanks. (The Soviet Union and its Warsaw Pact allies had tens of thousands of tanks deployed along the East-European frontier. In any European combat scenario, the United States and the nations of Western Europe would have had to be able to defeat these tanks.)

To meet this threat, the United States developed (and continues to develop) many antitank weapons. These include shoulder-fired anti-tank weapons, large-caliber recoilless rifles, aircraft-delivered missiles and bombs, smart munitions, and several other systems. No U.S. aircraft, however, carried a gun system capable of defeating Soviet tanks.

The Flyoff Competition

In 1967 the U.S. Air Force solicited proposals from twenty-one companies to build a prototype A-X aircraft. After evaluating all of the proposals, it selected Northrop and Fairchild Republic as contenders to enter the final phase of the competition. As part of a new procurement policy, it funded both companies to develop aircraft meeting the A-X specifications. After Northrop and Fairchild finished building the prototypes, the air force conducted extensive tests prior to making a decision.

During the competition, Northrop teamed with Ford Aerospace

Figure 23. A tank struck by GAU-8/A ammunition from the A-10 Thunderbolt. The GAU-8/A ammunition includes a mix of high explosive and depleted uranium projectiles.

and Communications Company. Ford built the gun used in the Northrop aircraft, which was designated the A-9. Unfortunately for both Northrop and Ford, the Ford gun experienced many problems during the test program, including blowing up on at least one occasion. The antitank gun was the primary weapon for the A-X aircraft, and because the Ford gun (which was also based on the Gatling principle) performed poorly, the outlook for the Northrop A-9 was bleak.

Fairchild Republic teamed with the General Electric Armament Division to build the A-10. The A-10 carried a new 30mm version of the Gatling gun named the "Avenger," which was based on the older 20mm Vulcan but was much more powerful. When General Electric became involved with the A-X program, it had nearly twenty years of development and production history with Gatling guns of various configurations. This experience was apparent during the test program, and the 30mm Avenger performed superbly. The A-10 rapidly demonstrated that it was a superior aircraft. The prototype flyoff competition

Figure 24. The GAU-8/A 30mm Gatling gun. The size and power of the Avenger cannon are obvious in this photograph.

ended in late 1972, and the A-10 was selected for a planned production run of six hundred aircraft.

The A-10 Thunderbolt II

The A-10 Thunderbolt II is unlike any aircraft in the U.S. inventory. It is quite unconventional in appearance when compared to other tactical jet aircraft, and for good reason. One notably different aspect of the A-10 is its unswept wings. The stubby wings are straight to allow flying at the very low speeds required for the close-air-support role. Another striking difference is the location of the engines, which are mounted high above the rear fuselage. There are two reasons for this. One is better protection from enemy small-arms fire. Another is that the rear fuselage masks the engines' heat signature, providing better protection from heat-seeking missiles.

The Gatling
Gun: 19th
Century
Machine Gun
to 21st
Century
Vulcan

88

The A-10 has many other unique features that are not as readily apparent. One is a high degree of component and subassembly interchangeability. To the maximum extent possible, left and right components of the aircraft are identical, which considerably reduces the number of spare parts needed to support it. The interchangeable components include the engines, landing gear, rudders, and many parts of the wings and tail. The landing gear design is also unique in that when it is retracted, the main and nose wheels protrude slightly beyond the outline of the fuselage. This permits the A-10 to make emergency gear-up landings without damage.

The A-10 is designed to survive small-arms fire. Control cables and hydraulic lines are routed so that one projectile could not inflict enough damage to make the aircraft unflyable. Another survivability feature is the cockpit design. The lower portion is surrounded by lightweight titanium armor to protect the pilot.

The A-10 payload is quite impressive. In addition to 30mm ammunition, the A-10 can carry missiles, bombs, cluster bombs, and other munitions, for a total of up to 18,500 pounds of ordnance. This is approximately equal to the weight of the aircraft, and is about double the payload of other aircraft used in the close-air-support role.

Yet the A-10's most intriguing feature is undoubtedly its 30mm Avenger Gatling gun.

The World's Most Powerful Gatling Gun

The heart of the A-10 is its 30mm gun. The military designation for this gun is the GAU-8/A (the GAU is pronounced "gow," and is an acronym for Gun, Automatic, Utility), and the A-10 was literally designed around it. The GAU-8/A is a seven-barreled 30mm Gatling gun that weighs approximately 3,900 pounds fully loaded (or about 20 percent of the total aircraft weight). The gun is hydraulically driven and is fed through a double helix drum and ammunition feed system similar to that of the 20mm Vulcan (more on the feed and storage system later).

One way to appreciate the power of this gun system is to consider it in relation to the A-10. The gun is mounted to place the firing barrel on the exact centerline of the aircraft, and for good reason. When firing at the maximum rate of 4,200 RPM (it can also fire at a reduced rate of 2,100 RPM), the GAU-8/A generates about 19,000 pounds of recoil. To put this in perspective, consider the power of the A-10's two fan turbine engines. Each of these generates about 9,000 pounds of thrust. When both engines are at full throttle, they generate a combined thrust of 18,000 pounds, which is less than the recoil of the GAU-8/A. In other words, when firing at maximum rate, more recoil force is generated by the GAU-8/A than by both of the engines operating at full throttle! The effect is quite noticeable, as the gun actually slows the A-10 when it is firing.

The high recoil of the GAU-8/A gun is also the reason the firing barrel is along the aircraft centerline. If it were not, the A-10 would turn away from the target each time the gun fired. Aircraft carrying the 20mm Vulcan in an off-centerline position are also susceptible to this phenomenon, but the recoil of the 20mm gun is small enough to allow for compensation by offsetting the rudder a few degrees. This is normally programed into the flight-control computer and requires no action by the pilot. That approach would not work on the A-10, though. The GAU-8/A gun simply generates too much recoil.

The GAU-8/A Gun System

The GAU-8/A Gun System is made up of four subsystems: the gun, the ammunition feed and storage subsystem, the drive subsystem, and the electrical control subsystem. Specifications for the GAU-8/A gun system are presented in Table 11-1 and explained below.

Table 11-1
GAU-8/A Gun System Specifications

Gun type:	7-barrel Gatling
Ammunition:	30mm HEI, TP, API
Firing rate:	4,200 or 2,100 spm
Gun system weight (loaded):	3,867 pounds
Gun system weight (unloaded):	1,861 pounds
Gun weight:	661 pounds
Drum weight:	780 pounds
Capacity:	1,200 rounds (drum); 1,350 rounds (system)
Drive:	hydraulic
Gun length:	112.83 inches
Barrel length:	93.1 inches
Clearing:	reverse rotation
Peak recoil:	19,000 pounds

GAU-8/A Gun

The GAU-8/A gun is a seven-barrel Gatling-based automatic cannon (see Figure 25). The gun subsystem consists of the following nine major components:

Rotor assembly. The rotor assembly is made up of the forward rotor (which accepts the barrels and is geared to the gun drive shaft) and the mid-rotor (to which the bolt guide tracks are mounted). The rotor assembly operates in the same manner and provides the same functions as that of other Gatling guns.

Housing. The housing serves as the basic frame of the GAU-8/A and provides a mount for many of the gun components (including the lubricator, ammunition transfer unit, solenoid assembly, firing cam, rotor, and other components). It also contains the elliptical cam path that drives the bolts back and forth.

Barrels. The GAU-8/A has seven barrels. Each is 93.1 inches long and has 20-groove right-hand constant twist rifling (unlike the 20mm Vulcan, which uses a gain twist rifling pattern).

Bolts. Seven bolts are used on the GAU-8/A. They are similar to those used on the 20mm Vulcan, except they are much larger and use a percussion (instead of an electrical) firing system.

Transfer unit. The transfer unit is mounted to the right side of the

Figure 25. The GAU-8/A cannon and ammunition. This seven-barreled Gatling gun fires several types of 30mm ammunition. The ammunition has an aluminum cartridge case, nylon rotating bands (to increase projectile velocity and decrease barrel wear), and (in the tank-busting role) a depleted uranium penetrator warhead.

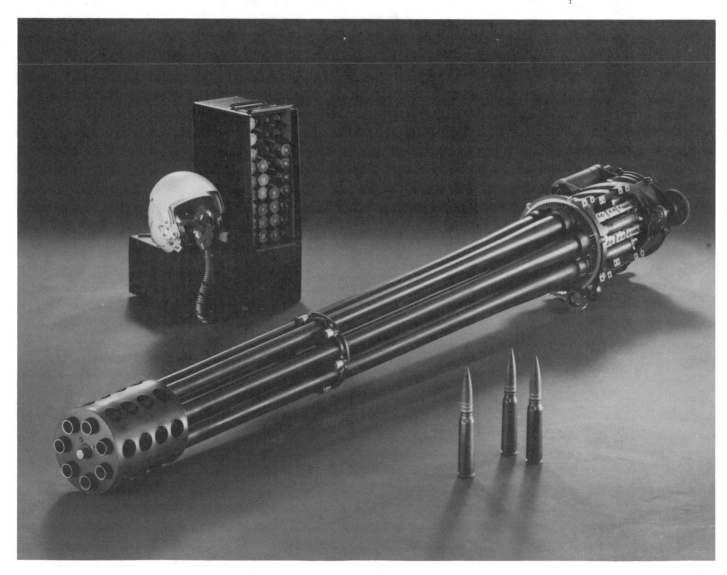

housing. It feeds ammunition into the gun and accepts fired and unfired cases from it.

Lubricator. The lubricator is mounted on the upper rear portion of the housing. It contains a reservoir of lubricant, and each time the gun fires a small quantity is injected onto the bolt tracks.

Solenoid assembly. The solenoid assembly is also mounted on the housing and is used to withdraw the firing pin safety when the firing signal is sent to the gun.

Mid-barrel support and clamp. The mid-barrel support and clamp provides the forward mounting point for the GAU-8/A. It also locks the barrels in position within the rotor.

Muzzle clamp. The muzzle clamp provides structural support for the cannon and maintains concentricity of the barrel cluster.

Ammunition Feed and Storage Subsystem

The ammunition feed and storage subsystem is used to store and convey live and spent rounds (empty cartridges are not ejected out of the A-10). The nine major components of the subsystem are as follows:

Ammunition storage drum. The ammunition storage drum is similar in concept to the drum used for the 20mm Vulcan. It consists of an inner and outer drum, two scoop-disk assemblies, two drum-cover assemblies, and two spacer rings. The inner drum has a double-helix that forces the rounds forward or backward when the inner drum is rotated. Ammunition passes through the drum-cover assemblies for loading, unloading, firing, and returning fired cartridge cases to the drum.

Entrance unit. The entrance unit is mounted on the rear drum-cover assembly. It receives fired cases from the conveyor elements (explained below) and passes them into the ammunition storage drum.

Exit unit. The exit unit is similar in concept to the entrance unit. It mounts on the front of the ammunition storage drum and is used to feed live rounds into the conveyor elements.

Ammunition chuting. The ammunition chuting provides a path for the conveyor elements that carry ammunition to and from the GAU-8/A gun.

Conveyor turnaround unit. The conveyor turnaround unit feeds live rounds into the gun transfer unit (explained in the description of the gun subsystem). The conveyor turnaround unit also accepts spent rounds from the gun transfer unit and places them in conveyor elements for return to the ammunition storage drum.

Ammunition conveyor elements. The ammunition conveyor elements are linked together to form an endless belt that travels to and from the gun through the ammunition chuting. Each element carries one round of ammunition going to the gun and one spent case or unfired round when returning to the ammunition storage drum.

Drum drive unit. Mounted on the drum exit cover, the drum drive unit drives the ammunition storage drum.

Equalizer. The equalizer is mounted on the ammunition chuting approximately midway between the ammunition storage drum and the GAU-8/A gun subsystem. It equalizes the tension between the feed and return ammunition conveyor elements.

Loading access unit. The loading access unit is used to load ammunition into the storage drum. It is accessible through a panel on the left side of the A-10 (just forward of the wing).

Drive Subsystem

The drive subsystem is a hydraulic drive assembly consisting of the following major components.

Hydraulic drive motors. Two identical hydraulic drive motors provide power for the GAU-8/A gun and the ammunition feed and storage system.

Accessory drive gearbox. The accessory drive gearbox is driven by the hydraulic drive motors. It provides output torque for the gun and drum drive shafts.

Gun drive shaft. The gun drive shaft provides power to the GAU-8/A gun subsystem.

Drum drive shaft. The drum drive shaft provides power to the ammunition feed and storage subsystem.

Electronic Control Subsystem

The electronic control subsystem consists of the electronic control unit. This "black box" contains the circuitry that controls all GAU-8/A logic functions.

System Operation

When the A-10 pilot engages a target, the first step is to bring the armament control system to a state of operational readiness. Once this is done, the pilot must get the target in the Heads Up Display screen, commonly referred to as the HUD. The HUD is a transparent screen mounted directly in the pilot's line of sight. A small pipper (or bright spot) is projected onto the screen, and the pilot maneuvers the airplane (and consequently, the GAU-8/A gun) until the pipper is directly on the target. This allows the pilot to engage the target without having to divert his vision. This capability is critically important in a close-air-support aircraft, which must fly at low altitudes.

When the pilot wants to fire the GAU-8/A gun, he presses the control-column-mounted trigger. The trigger sends a signal to the electronic control assembly, which subsequently sends a signal to two solenoids mounted on the hydraulic drive assembly. When these solenoids open, aircraft hydraulic pressure is applied to the two hydraulic drive motors, and the gun, ammunition storage drum, and chuting begin to move.

One-tenth of a second later, the electronic control assembly sends another signal to the firing solenoid assembly, which is mounted on the gun housing. This solenoid withdraws the safing sector from the firing cam path in the gun housing, which allows ammunition to begin the classic seven-step Gatling firing sequence. Each round fires as it reaches the firing point.

When the trigger is released, the electronic control assembly sends a reverse signal to the hydraulic drive assembly. The hydraulic drive motors reverse and rapidly decelerate the gun system. The gun system cycles in a reverse direction until all rounds are cleared from the cannon. This is done to prevent a cook-off (the inadvertent firing of a round due to absorption of residual gun heat), which could occur if a live round remained in one of the GAU-8/A's chambers.

The 30mm Family of Ammunition

The success story behind the 30mm family of ammunition used in the A-10 is as intriguing as the story behind the A-10 and the GAU-8/A. When the air force began the A-X program, the intent was to manufacture the 30mm ammunition in government arsenals. In the past, the government usually bought ammunition components from several suppliers and then did the loading, assembly, and packing operations in a government load plant. In the early 1970s, the government estimated that the cost of each 30mm round would be about seventy-five dollars.

Aerojet Ordnance Company and Honeywell, Inc. (two munitions manufacturers) convinced the government that it would be best to allow private industry to manufacture the complete round. Under this procurement concept, GAU-8/A ammunition production has been enormously successful. Private industry was able to deliver high-quality ammunition at about six dollars per round instead of the seventy-five the government originally planned to spend. To date, more than 80 million rounds have been procured. The 30mm family of ammunition consists of three different rounds, as explained below:

Target practice. The target practice (TP) cartridge is used for training. Essentially a slug, the projectile has an aluminum nose and steel body.

High-explosive incendiary. The high-explosive incendiary (HEI) cartridge fires an explosive warhead with a point-detonating fuze. The projectile body is made of steel and contains .124 pounds of a high explosive and incendiary mix.

Armor-piercing incendiary tracer. The armor-piercing incendiary tracer (APIT) cartridge fires what is probably the most intriguing of the 30mm projectiles. The APIT projectile has a depleted uranium penetrator sheathed in an aluminum sabot. The depleted uranium penetrator has two functions. Because depleted uranium is a very dense metal, it defeats enemy armor through kinetic energy alone (the combination of high velocity and mass allow it to break through armor). Depleted uranium is also pyrophoric, meaning it burns with intense heat after it breaks up. These two characteristics make it extremely effective against enemy tanks. The rear of the projectile contains a pyrotechnic fumer, which reduces aerodynamic drag and allows it to maintain high velocities.

The normal GAU-8/A combat mix of ammunition consists of one HEI round for every five APIT rounds (TP ammunition is used solely for target practice and is not usually mixed with HEI or APIT ammunition). All types of 30mm GAU-8/A ammunition use aluminum cartridge cases (to conserve weight) and either plastic or copper projectile bands (to engage the rifling in the GAU-8/A gun barrels). The projectile bands permit higher muzzle velocity and reduced barrel wear.

The Bottom Line

All things considered, the GAU-8/A 30mm Gatling gun is one of the most interesting and successful applications of ground-attack aircraft ever developed. The GAU-8/A gun system is the most powerful Gatling gun ever built. The extremely lethal 30mm family of ammunition is an amazing procurement success story. The A-10, the GAU-8/A, and the 30mm family of ammunition still make up an important part of the U.S. national defense and will continue to for quite some time.

12 The Vulcan Air Defense System

*T*he convoy ambled down the Vietnamese road, the dozen 2 1/2-ton trucks feeling their way cautiously along the muddy jungle trail. It was hot and humid—and dangerous. It was 1967 and the enemy was active. Two convoys had been ambushed recently on the same road and in the same area. Both had been escorted by M113 Armored Personnel Carriers with .50-caliber machine guns, but the APCs were the only vehicles to survive the ambush.

Today, however, the escort was unusual. The trucks were accompanied by two M163 Self-Propelled Vulcans, the army's latest experimental weapon. The new tracked vehicles looked strange, with their six-barreled Gatling guns appearing to be throwbacks to distant wars fought by the same army.

Suddenly, the jungle erupted in small-arms fire as Vietcong infantrymen sprayed the convoy with AK-47 fire. Two truck drivers were killed instantly, but before their trucks stopped rolling, the Vulcan turrets swung toward the enemy fire. Both Vulcans started firing at 1,000 RPM, enveloping the jungle with 20mm high-explosive warheads. Vietcong screams could be heard intermittently as the Vulcans roared and then paused, the gunners surveying the results of each burst prior to firing again. The sound of crashing tree trunks added to the fury, as the tree line moved steadily away from the convoy. The enemy small-arms fire subsided, and two Vietcong survivors scurried back to report the new weapon. The lesson was a costly one for the Vietcong, but they learned well. It was the first and only time a Vulcan-escorted convoy would be ambushed in Vietnam.

Near the end of World War II, the need for a new aircraft gun system began to take shape. The artillery branch of the U.S. Army, which was responsible for antiaircraft ground-based gun systems, recognized the need for a gun system with greater capabilities for the same reasons that eventually led to the development of the Vulcan cannon: the advent of faster, less-vulnerable jet aircraft that could be defeated only with higher rates of fire and explosive projectiles.

The army's approach to ground-based air defense took two forms at the end of World War II. For low-flying aircraft, the approach was to provide saturation fire with the quad .50 machine gun mount. This weapon consisted of four .50-caliber Browning machine guns mounted on a turret. The quad .50 used a manual tracking system. For higher-flying targets, larger gun systems were used with explosive projectiles. The warheads fired by these gun systems could be fired in either a point-detonating mode (i.e., direct contact with the target) or an altitude mode. The altitude mode detonated the warhead at a preselected height, creating a "flak" field that—it was hoped—would defeat the target aircraft.

The Gatling
Gun: 19th
Century
Machine Gun
to 21st
Century
Vulcan

96

Neither of these systems were expected to be very effective against the new jet threat. Flak-based antiaircraft fire was only marginally effective during World War II, and the quad .50 machine gun was generally recognized to be inadequate as an antiaircraft weapon.

Gun-based air defense against anything other than low-altitude targets largely disappeared with the advent of missiles. Missiles could be directed against high- and medium-altitude enemy aircraft by radar or infrared guidance systems. The low-altitude threat remained, though, and was considered particularly critical for forward ground combat units. The army needed an air defense system that offered a quick response time, required relatively low technology, and was highly mobile. All of these requirements favored gun systems over missiles.

The army's first weapon system to respond to these requirements was the M42 Duster. The Duster utilized off-the-shelf components to the maximum extent possible (which, as will be discussed later, would be the case when the Vulcan Air Defense System was developed). The M42's twin 40mm gun system was taken from the navy, which had used the mount with some success to defend ships against low-altitude aircraft during World War II. The chassis was a modified M41 Walker Bulldog tank.

The M42 Duster was first fielded in the 1950s, and incredibly, it is still in use with some forces today (the Taiwanese army and the New Mexico Army National Guard). One of the secrets of the M42's longevity is its amazing effectiveness against lightly armored ground targets. The U.S. Army used Dusters extensively in Vietnam in this application, particularly for convoy escort duty and for moving tree lines away from artillery base camps. The New Mexico National Guard even used its Dusters once to assist in rounding up prisoners in the New Mexico wilderness after a mass escape from a state prison.

As the U.S. Army entered the 1960s, it was left with the M42 Duster and the quad .50 machine gun mount as its primary defense against low-altitude aircraft. Both systems had serious disadvantages against the modern air threat. Neither had a radar-directed fire-control system, which was thought to be essential against high-speed, low-altitude targets. Neither could deliver saturation fire (and in effect, form a shot pattern in much the same manner as a shotgun does against a bird). The M42 used a gasoline engine at a time when the army wanted all of its tactical vehicles to be diesel powered, and it suffered the added disadvantage of being heavy. It was not helicopter-transportable, and during this era, the army was basing much of its new high-mobility doctrine on the use of the helicopter. Finally, the M42 could not be air-dropped, which meant neither of the army's two airborne divisions could use it.

For these reasons, in the early 1960s the army made a decision to pursue a new gun-based low-altitude air defense system. After studying the problem, it decided two systems were needed. One should be a very lightweight version capable of helicopter transport or parachute delivery. The other was to be mounted on the army's standard lightweight tracked vehicle (the M113 armored personnel carrier). The army specified that both systems must have radar-directed fire-control systems, as well as gun systems based on the 20mm M61 Vulcan cannon.

General Electric's Armament Division in Burlington, Vermont, was awarded a contract to develop two working prototype air defense systems based on the above requirements. In 1964 and 1965, the two systems it developed were tested successfully against aerial targets at Fort Bliss, Texas, home of the U.S. Army's Air Defense Center and School. Testing continued, and in 1968 the Vulcan Air Defense System (VADS) became a standard army weapon system.

At one point, and as part of the test program, a small team of Self-Propelled Vulcans went to Vietnam for a six-month combat evaluation. The Vulcans were never used against enemy aircraft, as the United States generally enjoyed air superiority over South Vietnam and there were no enemy aircraft to shoot at. The Vulcans were used in a ground-to-ground role, however, and they were extremely successful. The Vulcans were ambushed just one time during a convoy escort mission, with disastrous consequences for the enemy. During the remainder of their tour in Vietnam, the Vulcans were never fired upon (thus fulfilling Dr. Gatling's 1865 vision of a weapon system so awesome no enemy would dare engage it).

M163 Self-Propelled Vulcan

One of the requirements for the development of the Vulcan Air Defense System was that it utilize off-the-shelf components to the maximum extent possible. The M163 Self-Propelled Vulcan satisfied this requirement. The M163 was a marriage of two major systems: the existing M113 Armored Personnel Carrier and the Vulcan Air Defense System turret. The M163 Self-Propelled Vulcan is shown in Figure 26.

The M113 Armored Personnel Carrier, built by FMC in San Jose, California, had become the army's standard tracked utility vehicle by the time the Vulcan Air Defense System was under development.

The Gatling
Gun: 19th
Century
Machine Gun
to 21st
Century
Vulcan

98

Surprisingly few modifications were required for General Electric to mount the Vulcan Air Defense System turret. Among the obvious changes were a hole in the top of the hull to accept the Vulcan turret and suitable interior fixturing. Another modification was a suspension lockout system, which prevented the vehicle from rocking due to the gun's recoil. When the Vulcan was emplaced in a stationary position, the suspension lockout system maximized accuracy by providing a stable firing platform. The Vulcan could also be fired without locking the vehicle's suspension, however, which allowed the system to fire on the move.

Figure 26. The M163 Self-Propelled Vulcan. This system uses the 20mm M61 Gatling gun on a modified armored personnel carrier chassis in an air defense role. The system is also highly effective against ground targets.

The only other significant modification to the standard M113 was the addition of polystyrene flotation pods to the sides of the vehicle. The M113 is amphibious, but the waterline is fairly close to the top of the vehicle. With the added weight of the Vulcan Air Defense System turret, the flotation pods were necessary to add buoyancy and keep water from spilling into the crew hatches (they add only about 3 inches to the sides of the vehicle). With the incorporation of these changes, the M113 was designated the M741 gun carriage.

The Vulcan Air Defense System turret consists of four major subsystems:

- the M61A1 Vulcan 20mm cannon
- the turret and its controls

- the ammunition feed and stowage system
- the fire-control system

Figure 27. The Vulcan Air Defense System firing at night. The tracer pattern illustrates the concept of a shot pattern. Due to the high number of projectiles and the short period of time in which they are fired, the Vulcan can be more accurately thought of as a shotgun rather than a machine gun. Note that only every sixth round is a tracer.

The Vulcan cannon subsystem is quite similar to the one described in Chapter 8, with the major differences being the dispersion pattern and the rate of fire. Vulcans used in other applications use one muzzle clamp (the device that holds the six barrels together near the muzzle end). In the air defense application, two clamps are carried with each system, and they are interchangeable for different shot patterns. One provides a 6x18-mil elliptical shot pattern (used to cover a broad area), and the other provides a 6-mil circular dispersion pattern (used to provide concentrated firepower). Figure 27 shows a Vulcan firing tracer ammunition at night, providing a good visual presentation of the shot patterns discussed above. The muzzle clamps can be switched in less than five minutes.

In the air defense application, the rate of fire has been slowed from the normal 6,000 RPM used by aircraft-mounted Vulcans. The Vulcan Air Defense System gunner can select either 1,000 or 3,000 shots per minute.

99

The system will fire continuously at the 1,000 RPM rate. At the 3,000 RPM rate, it will fire a preselected burst of 10, 30, 60, or 100 rounds.

The second major subsystem is the turret and its controls. The turret is electrically driven by three solid-state servo-amplifiers, each of which is coupled to a direct-current motor. Two of these are used for turret azimuth drive, and one is used for elevation. All three are interchangeable, and the turret will drive in azimuth if only one of its two drive motors is working (although the azimuth slew rate will be slower). The turret can normally slew in azimuth at rates up to 60 degrees per second and in elevation at rates up to 45 degrees per second, and it can accelerate to these rates quickly. This high response rate offers the gunner and the Vulcan fire-control system the ability to track close and rapidly maneuvering targets.

The third major subsystem is the ammunition feed and stowage system, which is very similar to those used for aircraft applications, as explained in Chapter 9. The system consists of a 1,100-round storage drum and a linkless feed system. The linkless feed system is basically a conveyor, taking ammunition from the storage drum and delivering it to the gun. Once the ammunition has been cycled through the gun, empty cases or unfired rounds are tossed overboard. The linkless system eliminates the problems associated with defective or stretched links and provides for more reliable feeding. The storage drum has an internal double helix, and its principle of operation is very similar to the Accles feed described in Chapter 3. In addition to the 1,100 rounds of ready-to-fire ammunition, the Self-Propelled Vulcan can carry another 5,000 rounds in storage containers located beneath the bench seats in the rear of the vehicle. These additional rounds are linked (20mm ammunition is normally delivered to the military in this manner), and the ammunition must be fed through a delinking feeder to load it into the 1,100-round storage drum. Loading the drum takes about six minutes.

The fourth major subsystem, the fire-control system, consists of a set of sights, a sight current generator, and a range-only radar. Three sighting devices are available for use with the Vulcan. Two of these are intended for use against ground targets only, and the third can be used against both ground targets and aircraft. The two ground sights include a starlight night vision device and a daylight telescope. These are normally carried in a container inside the vehicle (they are installed when ground use is anticipated).

The third sighting device is the gyroscopic lead-computing gunsight, and in the air defense role it normally works in conjunction with the sight current generator and the range-only radar. This gunsight has a reticle located in a window. When any member of the crew sees an enemy aircraft, the gunner traverses and elevates the gun system until he sees the target in the reticle. Once this is done, he steps on a foot pedal that energizes the radar. While the gunner continues to move the turret (keeping the target aircraft in the reticle), the radar computes the range and velocity of the target. The system automatically compensates for air density through altitude and temperature inputs made by the crew. The radar then sends this information to the sight current generator, which computes the proper lead angle and elevation for the gun system. This signal is then sent to the gunsight. When this occurs, the gunner sees the reticle suddenly move to a new location in the gunsight window. When the gunner moves the turret to center the target in the displaced reticle, the Vulcan cannon will fire with the proper lead and elevation.

Aerial targets can also be engaged without using the radar. In the manual mode of operation, the gunner can estimate the range and velocity of the aircraft, make these inputs to the control panel, and the reticle will move as if directed by the radar. The accuracy of the system in the manual mode is dependent upon the accuracy of the gunner's estimates for range and velocity. Actual firings against airborne drones, however, have shown that gunners can provide accurate estimates consistently and defeat the target.

The lead-computing gun sight can also be used against ground targets simply by locking the reticle and centering the target in it. In practice, this is the mode in which most ground targets are engaged.

M167 Towed Vulcan

The M167 Towed Vulcan (shown in Figure 28) was designed for deployment with airborne and airmobile units. Airborne units use parachutes to drop into combat, and at only 3,000 pounds, the Towed Vulcan is capable of parachute delivery. Airmobile units use helicopters instead of parachutes, and the Towed Vulcan is light enough to be carried beneath the UH-1 series of Huey helicopters and other army utility helicopters.

There are three major differences between the M167 and M163 Vulcans. These are the carriage, the ammunition feed and stowage system, and the power system. These aside, the two Vulcans are basically identical.

The carriage is the most obvious difference between the two systems. Instead of using a modified M113 armored personnel carrier, the Towed Vulcan is mounted on a lightweight, two-wheeled gun carriage. The primary tow vehicle is the M561 Gama Goat (a 1 1/4-ton articulated utility vehicle), but the 2 1/2-ton M35 "Deuce-and-a-half" is also used. The M167 Vulcan can be towed at speeds up to 45 MPH and can ford streams up to 30 inches deep.

The second major difference between the two versions of the Vulcan Air Defense System is the ammunition feed and storage system. The Self-Propelled version uses a linkless feed and storage drum, as described above. To save weight, the Towed version uses linked ammunition suspended from rails in a 500-round storage container. The storage container is mounted on the left side of the turret, out of the gunner's line of sight. Additional ammunition is carried in the tow vehicle. The basic load for the Towed Vulcan is 4,000 rounds, but more can be carried in the towing vehicle.

The third difference is the power system. Both the Towed and Self-Propelled versions use 24-volt nickel-cadmium batteries. The Self-Propelled version uses three batteries. One provides power for turret fire control and drive, while the other two are connected to provide power for the ammunition feed system and the cannon. The Towed Vulcan, with its linked feed system, does not need the third battery to power the chuting and storage drum helix associated with the Self-Propelled version's linkless feed system. The method used to charge the batteries is also different. The Self-Propelled version uses the vehicle's charging circuit, while the Towed Vulcan relies on a separate gasoline-powered generator for this purpose. This generator is mounted on the front of the trailer

Figure 28. The M167 Towed Vulcan. This system is similar to the M163 Vulcan, except that it is a lightweight, Towed version designed for deployment with airborne and airmobile units.

and is used only when the Towed version's batteries require charging. Normally, both the Towed and Self-Propelled versions can remain in the standby mode for long periods of time, quietly ready to fire.

Ammunition

The Vulcan Air Defense System uses seven different types of 20mm ammunition, as described below. All are electrically primed, with the exception of the dummy round, which does not fire and uses no primer.

M51 dummy ammunition. The dummy round is used primarily for training. Dummy ammunition can be loaded into and cycled through both the Towed and Self-Propelled versions of the Vulcan Air Defense System.

M55A2 target practice ammunition. TP ammunition is also used primarily for training. Target practice ammunition launches an inert projectile at a muzzle velocity of approximately 3,300 fps.

M220 target practice tracer ammunition. TP-T ammunition is similar to TP ammunition, except that it contains a tracer element.

M56A3 high-explosive incendiary ammunition. HEI ammunition contains both a high-explosive charge and an incendiary element for starting fires. The projectile contains a point-detonating fuze to detonate the warhead.

M246 high-explosive incendiary tracer/self-destruct ammunition. HEIT-SD ammunition is similar to HEI, except that it contains both a tracer element and a self-destruct feature. This ammunition was developed specifically for the air-defense application. The tracer element allows the gunner to compensate for aiming errors, and the self-destruct feature prevents live high-explosive projectiles from landing on friendly troops.

M52 armor-piercing incendiary ammunition. API ammunition is designed to overcome lightly armored vehicles. Each round contains a tungsten penetrator, which is a very dense metal and defeats the target through its high kinetic energy (i.e., a dense mass moving at high velocity, which breaks through armor). Each round also contains an incendiary element to start fires.

M52 armor-piercing incendiary tracer ammunition. API-T ammunition is similar to API, except that it contains a tracer element.

Organization

The M163 Self-Propelled Vulcan is normally deployed in a composite Chaparral/Vulcan battalion (Chaparral is a self-propelled air-defense system that uses a modified version of the Sidewinder missile). This type of battalion is usually deployed with armor and infantry divisions (except for airborne or airmobile divisions) and consists of a headquarters battery, two Chaparral batteries, and two Vulcan batteries. Each Vulcan battery contains twelve Self-Propelled Vulcans, organized into three platoons, each having four Vulcans. The 82nd Airborne and 101st Airmobile Divisions have similar air defense battalions, except that in these divisions, Towed Vulcans replace both the Chaparrals and the Self-Propelled and 220 Towed Vulcans.

Future of the Vulcan Air Defense System

The Vulcan Air Defense System will be with the U.S. Army (as well as other military forces) for a long time. There are several reasons for this, but the one requiring immediate comment is the advent and demise of the Sergeant York DIVAD Gun System, shown in Figure 29.

Figure 29. The Sergeant York DIVAD System. This ill-fated system, intended to replace the M163 Vulcan Air Defense System, was ultimately dropped due to its inability to meet performance requirements. DIVAD relied on twin 40mm Bofors cannons instead of a Gatling gun.

DIVAD (an acronym for Divisional Air Defense) was designed to be a replacement for the M163 Self-Propelled Vulcan. The system used twin 40mm Bofors cannons instead of Vulcan's 20mm General Electric Gatling-based gun system. The DIVAD gun carriage was based on the M48 tank chassis instead of the M113 armored personnel carrier. The 40mm round offered obvious range and lethality advantages. DIVAD also had other features that should have made it a better weapon than the Self-Propelled Vulcan. These included an acquisition radar, a feature to identify whether aircraft are friendly or hostile, state-of-the-art electronics, and other classified features.

During development, however, the DIVAD demonstrated serious deficiencies. As troops in the field know only too well, increased complexity generally translates into decreased reliability, and it proved true in this case. The DIVAD development program also had severe cost overruns, and the army claimed it did not meet all of its performance requirements. This attracted criticism from both the U.S. military and Congress.

DIVAD was never a candidate for replacing the Towed Vulcan. Even if it could have overcome the problems described above, the 82nd Airborne and the 101st Airmobile Divisions still would have required Towed Vulcans. The army ultimately cancelled the DIVAD program.

The U.S. Army experimented with improved versions of the basic Vulcan Air Defense System, the most noteworthy of these projects being the PIVADS program. Although the acronym is strikingly similar to DIVAD, in this case it stood for Product Improved Vulcan Air Defense System. Lockheed Electronics was the prime contractor (this organization ultimately went out of business, however). Lockheed's improvement efforts focused on three areas: improved response (attained through the use of faster computers and better servomotors), improved target acquisition (made possible by an improved sight that allowed the gunner to control the reticle), and improved target tracking (achieved by allowing a computer, instead of the gunner, to move the turret). The army tested PIVADS at Fort Bliss, Texas, with satisfying results.

General Electric has done a great deal of work to find new applications for the Vulcan Air Defense System, and it has successfully marketed the turret in other mounts. One of these is the GE/Cadillac-Gage Commando Air Defense System, which has been sold to Saudi Arabia. This system consists of the M167 Towed Vulcan turret mounted on the Cadillac-Gage V-150 wheeled armored vehicle. This system may also be sold to other nations.

The Blazer was another General Electric Gatling-based system used as a development test bed. General Electric initiated work on this Gatling-based air defense system in 1985. The Blazer mounted a

25mm five-barreled GAU-12/U gun and four Stinger air defense missiles on the army's new Bradley Fighting Vehicle (which is replacing the M113 armored personnel carrier). Blazer offered several advantages, including improved lethality from the 25mm gun, built-in test and diagnostic equipment, an IFF capability (IFF stands for identification friend or foe), a search and acquisition radar, and multiple target engagement capability. Blazer also had a fully stabilized firing platform, which allowed its 25mm Gatling gun to accurately engage targets while the system was on the move.

As a direct result of the Blazer program's success, the U.S. Marine Corps contracted with General Electric in 1987 for the full-scale engineering development of two Light Armored Vehicle-Air Defense (LAV-AD) systems. The LAV-AD (shown in Figure 30) is a truly impressive weapon system. In addition to mounting the GAU-12/U 25mm Gatling gun on an eight-wheeled combat vehicle (the Marine Corps' Piranha), the LAV-AD also mounts Stinger antiaircraft missiles and Hydra 70 rockets. The LAV-AD sensor suite includes forward-looking infrared radar, a television, and an eye-safe laser rangefinder.

Other 20mm Gatling-based weapon systems in the U.S. military have been the subject of experimental "upgun" programs, and although the army has no current plans, it is not inconceivable that at some point in the future there will be an upgunned Vulcan Air Defense System. An upgun program, which would be indicated in the event that the weapon system's primary target becomes more difficult to defeat, would consist of feasibility studies and tests to assess replacing the 20mm gun with a 25mm or 30mm version.

Even if the army decided to retire all of its Vulcan Air Defense Systems from frontline active duty (which is extremely unlikely), the New Mexico National Guard

Figure 30. The General Electric Light Armored Vehicle Air Defense System. This system is based on the GE GAU-12/U 25mm Gatling gun. The system also has General Dynamics Stinger Missiles and a variety of target acquisition and tracking features. It is mounted on the Marine Corps' Piranha vehicle.

would probably replace its aging but well-maintained M42 Dusters with Vulcans. Based on this, as well as the factors discussed above, it is clear that the Vulcan Air Defense System and its derivatives will be strong contributors to our national defense for many years to come.

13 The Phalanx Close-In Weapon System

*T*he sailor was nervous. Duty in the Persian Gulf had always been tense, but the events of the last few hours had made the tension all but unbearable. The USS New Jersey, *the ship underneath the sailor, was facing the gravest danger she had ever seen in her fifty years of service. The ship's bridge was air-conditioned against the 100-degree-plus temperatures outside, but the sailor was perspiring. He noticed that his shipmates were, too. The naval intelligence briefing had warned of the Iraqi sea-skimming missiles (that copied an American design stolen from the U.S. producer). Air cover was practically useless against such a threat, as the missiles flew at nearly supersonic speeds only a few feet above the waves, rendering aircraft radars useless. Only one weapon could defend the* New Jersey *now: the Phalanx guns at each of the ship's four corners.*

The sailor was a radar technician, and he knew that the Phalanx radar could pick up any sea-skimmers. What he didn't know was how the white-domed Phalanx system gun could possibly react in time to destroy a missile only a few hundred feet away from the ship. Although he had been a Phalanx technician for more than a year, he had never seen the mighty gun fired.

The sailor knew that the Phalanx was a fully automated system. Once armed and made operational, it searched for and fired at any low-flying incoming targets without operator input. The knowledge should have been comforting, but it only made the sailor cringe when he heard the system's servomotors energize and the giant white dome began to slew. He knew that meant it had picked up a target. He also know that either he and his shipmates or the target would be destroyed in the next few seconds.

In less than a second, the 20mm cannon erupted in a violent roar. Even though the sailor had anticipated the Vulcan bark, it startled him. It was just a short burst, not more than 100 rounds, but that was all it took. He felt the shock wave from the violent and brilliant explosion, not more than 500 feet away, as the sea-skimming missile's warhead detonated from the impact of the 20mm tungsten projectiles. Another bark from the New Jersey's *aft starboard Phalanx followed a second later, and the sailor saw a similar explosion at the ship's aft end. Before he could adjust his senses to recognize that the aft Phalanx had just defeated a second sea-skimming missile, the same thing occurred directly in from of him again, as the closest Phalanx defeated yet a third missile. The sailor couldn't even see the missiles, but in a heartbeat two Phalanx systems had done their jobs, defeating three lethal antiship missiles and saving the* New Jersey. *As men are known to do after escaping a danger so severe and rapid that they can scarcely comprehend its significance, the sailor laughed. He heard his crewmates in the* New Jersey's *bridge do the same.*

For many thousands of years, the only significant threat to a warship was another warship. As technology advanced, the family of threats grew to include guns and torpedoes. In World War II, the threat posed by aircraft became significant. Single-barreled antiaircraft gun systems from .50-caliber up to 40mm were employed to counter this threat. In the years since World War II, the airborne threat to surface vessels continued to move in the direction of sea-skimming supersonic aircraft, helicopters, and antiship missiles.

There is little argument today about what poses the deadliest threat to ships, and that is the antiship missile, particularly during its final low-level flight phase when it is the most difficult to detect and defeat. This is due to a combination of size (an incoming antiship missile presents a very small frontal profile), speed (many antiship missiles are supersonic), and lethality (antiship missiles carry enormously powerful shaped-charge warheads capable of defeating very thick armor).

The extent of the threat posed by antiship missiles probably was not appreciated fully until the 1967 Arab-Israeli War. In the war, an Egyptian Komar-class gunboat sank the Israeli destroyer *Eliath* with a single Styx missile. The navies of the world were again reminded of the threat when the Argentines sank the HMS *Sheffield* with one hit from an Exocet missile during the Falklands conflict. Today, the known threat includes no fewer than twenty-one different types of antiship missiles (and there are almost certainly covert antiship weapons of even greater capability).

Phalanx Development and Deployment

In the late 1960s, the U.S. Navy fully understood that its ships were inadequately equipped to counter the threat of antiship missiles, particularly those capable of penetrating the outer defense umbrella provided by the target ship's defensive missiles. In 1969, the Naval Sea Systems Command awarded a contract to the Pomona Division of General Dynamics to study this challenge. The objective of the study was to determine if a radar-directed, high-rate-of-fire gun system could provide an effective defense against close-in antiship missiles.

The General Dynamics study showed that the navy concept would work if the new close-in weapons system used a closed-loop spotting concept. The idea behind this system was that it would use the radar to locate not only the target, but also its own fired projectiles with respect to the target. In this manner, the gun system could correct for the miss distance and adjust the gun's aim to bring the projectiles onto the target.

The navy was pleased and funded General Dynamics to continue this work. General Dynamics continued to refine the closed-loop aiming technology. They fabricated a test unit and initiated testing in 1970. Ground tests were extremely successful. The next step was the Tactical Missile Test Program, which consisted of attacking a Phalanx-equipped, decommissioned ship (the USS *Cunningham*) with glide bombs and drones. The low-flying bombs and drones attacked using a variety of flight profiles in an attempt to penetrate the Phalanx defense (including extremely low-level, subsonic, supersonic, and stream attack). None of the attack profiles were successful. The Phalanx, named after an ancient Greek military formation of foot soldiers standing close together with overlapping shields and spears to create an impenetrable defense, was proving to be true to its name.

The test program continued, and in 1976 the Phalanx was installed on the USS *Bigelow* (an active-duty destroyer) for operational evaluation testing. The Phalanx performed superbly in all areas. All targets that flew against the *Bigelow* were destroyed with multiple hits. The Phalanx was shown to be an extremely reliable system (its reliability was four times better than the requirement), and its maintainability was also deemed superior (repair times were well below those specified by the navy).

As a result of the Phalanx' superior performance, the navy approved it for production in 1978 and deliveries began the next year. In 1980, the Phalanx system was installed on the USS *America*, the USS *Enterprise*, the USS *Coral Sea*, the USS *Biddle*, and the USS *England*. Aircraft carriers were the first to receive the system, primarily because of their value and their vulnerability (an aircraft carrier is a huge target). In 1981, seven additional U.S. Navy ships were armed with Phalanx systems.

Ultimately, thirty-five classes of U.S. ships, from frigates to aircraft carriers, will be equipped with a total of 260 Phalanx systems. In addition to those already installed on ships, nine Phalanx systems are installed at three U.S. Navy training centers. Phalanx is also highly favored by U.S. allies, including Great Britain, Australia, Japan, Saudi Arabia, and Pakistan. Great Britain was particularly anxious to procure the Phalanx after an Exocet missile sank the *Sheffield* in the Falklands. Not long after that unfortunate event, Britain installed Phalanx on two aircraft carriers, the HMS *Invincible* and the HMS *Illustrious*.

The Gatling
Gun: 19th
Century
Machine Gun
to 21st
Century
Vulcan

112

The Phalanx System

The Phalanx Close-In Weapon System consists of seven major subsystems:

- the fire control radar/servo assembly
- the electronic enclosure
- the local control console
- the remote control panel
- the barbette assembly
- the mount and drive assembly
- the 20mm gun assembly

Each of these is explained below.

Fire Control Radar/ Servo Assembly. The fire control radar/servo assembly includes both a search and a track radar. This subsystem both searches for and locks onto targets and determines range, azimuth, and velocity for both the target and the projectiles fired by the Phalanx 20mm cannon.

Electronic Enclosure. The electronic enclosure is mounted in the mount and train drive assembly. It includes most of the electronic circuit cards that govern operation of the Phalanx system.

Local Control Console. The local control console is mounted near, but not on, the Phalanx system. It includes a system test set, a power supply unit,

Figure 31. The Phalanx Close-In Weapon System. This system uses a 20mm M61 Gatling gun and is mounted on ships to protect them against antiship missiles.

and other electronics. The system allows the operator to control the Phalanx manually (i.e., it allows the operator to control the system in other than the fully automatic mode).

Remote Control Panel. The remote control panel allows system operation from remote locations. Using the remote control panel, the operator can control the system in the manual mode to engage surface targets.

Barbette Assembly. The barbette assembly mounts in the base of the Phalanx system. It contains other subassemblies that support Phalanx operation, including the hydraulic power supply, the radar transmitter and its power supply, a heat exchanger, transformers, and an environmental control unit.

Mount and Train Drive Assembly. The mount and train drive assembly provides the mount for the 20mm cannon and the white-domed fire control radar/servo assembly. It is the system's turret, allowing for radar and gun system elevation, depression, and traverse.

20mm Gun Assembly. The 20mm gun assembly is the heart of the Phalanx system. It uses the standard six-barreled 20mm Vulcan cannon, which is electrically controlled and hydraulically driven in the Phalanx application. Phalanx uses a helical storage drum and ammunition feed system that allows for a firing rate of 3,000 RPM. After firing, each empty cartridge case is returned to the rear of the storage drum (taking the place of fired rounds). This keeps the ship's deck clear of fired cases.

Follow-On Gatling-Based Close-In Weapon Systems

Based on the success of the Phalanx system, several variants have been or are being developed. One such system is the Goalkeeper, which is a joint General Electric/Hollandse Signaalapparaten BV (a Dutch company) system based on the 30mm GAU-8/A cannon (details on the GAU-8/A are included in Chapter 11). Both Britain and the Netherlands have an interest in the Goalkeeper system. The Netherlands has already armed several of its ships with Goalkeepers.

Although no details are available, the Russians even have a Gatling-based ship defense system. It's called the ADG6-30. Beyond that, little else is known.

After the Falklands crisis, in which an Exocet missile sank the British *Sheffield*, the United States took a great interest in upgunning its Phalanx systems. Studies were performed to evaluate the feasibility of converting to a 25mm Gatling and incorporating a 20mm depleted uranium penetrator round. These efforts and studies continue to this day.

14 Pod-Mounted Gatling Guns

*T*he F-4 pilot felt like a kid playing cowboys and Indians—like he was wearing two Colt .45s in tooled leather holsters. The analogy was not so farfetched. The two externally mounted 30mm Gatling gun pods (one under each wing) were considerably more firepower than he was used to carrying. The mission required it, though. He was on patrol in the Saudi desert, flying low against the sand, prepared to engage any armored columns that dared stray in from occupied Kuwait.

"Lima Bean 6, this is Lima Bean 1," the pilot heard on his radio. "We have a report of a column of T-62s approximately 20 miles east of your location. Ground forces are engaging; they are requesting close air support."

"On the way," the pilot keyed in, as he pushed the two throttles to afterburner. In seconds, the big F-4 was just below the sound barrier, and in minutes, he saw the combatants on the desert floor below. None of the tanks had been stopped; all were moving west, headed into Saudi Arabia.

The pilot hit the master arm switch, and after noting that no ZSU-23/4 antiaircraft vehicles accompanied the column ("either out of arrogance or stupidity," he thought), he climbed to 2,500 feet and began his strafing run. At 700 feet above ground level and at a slant range of about 2,000 feet, he fired a 30-round burst from each pod. He felt the aircraft sway right and then left as the recoil from the big 30mm cannons gently rocked it. He pulled up and over for an inverted look at the column.

The pilot smiled. All of the vehicles had stopped, and five of the seven were burning. "One more satisfied customer," he thought. He considered making another pass to light up the remaining two vehicles, but he knew that the ground forces could finish them off, and he needed to conserve both ammunition and fuel. He knew there would be other columns to engage before the patrol was over.

In addition to the numerous aircraft-, ship-, and vehicle-mounted Gatling guns discussed thus far, General Electric has also developed several pod-mounted Gatling guns. These gun pods allow virtually any aircraft that can carry external stores the capability to fly with a Gatling gun. The General Electric gun pod systems are available in three calibers: 7.62mm, 20mm, and 30mm. The McDonnell Douglas AV-8B Harrier also utilizes a unique pod-mounted approach for its 25mm GAU-12/U cannon, which will be explained below.

20mm Gatling Gun Pods

General Electric builds two variants of the 20mm gun pod. The first is the SUU-16/A Vulcan Gun Pod, which utilizes a ram air-powered version of the M-61 20mm Vulcan cannon. (A brief explanation of the terminology used to describe aircraft external stores is perhaps in order: "SUU" is an abbreviation for suspension unit, which simply means that the device is suspended externally from an aircraft. The numerical designation, in this case 16, simply denotes the model. The "/A" configuration denotes that the system stays with the aircraft and is not released in use. Bombs that are released from the aircraft are designated with "/B," e.g., the SUU-65/B tactical munitions dispenser.)

The second 20mm pod-mounted Gatling gun is the SUU-23/A Vulcan Gun Pod (see Figures 32 and 33). This is a particularly interesting variant of the basic 20mm Vulcan, in that gases generated by the 20mm ammunition are used to drive the gun (this version of the M-61 is designated the GAU-4).

The SUU-23/A's six-barreled GAU-4/A cannon initially relies on a small electric motor to start the barrel cluster (the motor can accelerate the gun system to a firing rate in excess of 5,000 RPM in about two-tenths of a second). After that, propellant gases from the firing 20mm ammunition are bled from the barrels and fed into a piston and cam mechanism that drives the gun, accelerating it to 6,000 RPM.

The SUU-23/A is most commonly used on the F-4D Phantom,

Figure 32. The U.S. Air Force SUU-23/A 20mm Vulcan Gun Pod, which is also used by the U.S. Army (as the M-25) in certain helicopter and fixed-wing applications. The system has a six-barreled gun-gas-driven 20mm Vulcan. General Electric also offers a ram-air-driven version denoted as the SUU-16/A (in U.S. Air Force applications) and the M-12 (in U.S. Army applications).

Figure 33. A 20mm Vulcan gun pod firing from the experimental Northrop F-20 Tigershark. The F-20 was a Northrop-funded fighter development program that failed to achieve commercial success.

although it can be used on other tactical aircraft (recall from Chapter 9 that the F-4E carries an internally mounted 20mm M-61 Gatling gun). The SUU-23/A dispenser can carry 1,200 rounds of 20mm ammunition, and it weighs about 1,700 pounds fully loaded. The system mounts on standard U.S. 30-inch aircraft external store lugs, which are compatible with the U.S. Century Series and other fighters.

Mini-Gun Pods

General Electric also has pod-mounted versions of its 7.62mm Gatling (the mini-gun). The 7.62mm pod-mounted Gatling gun is designated as the SUU-11B/A by the U.S. Air Force and the XM-18E1 by the U.S. Army. The army version is shown in Figure 34. The SUU-11B/A is the latest version (superseding both the earlier SUU-11/A and SUU-11A/A versions for the air force). The difference between the current version of this system and its predecessors is that it can fire at either of two rates (the earlier versions could only fire at one). The Air Force SUU-11B/A can fire at either 3,000 or 6,000 shots per minute, while the Army XM-18E1 can fire at either 2,000 or 4,000 shots per minute. Both systems can carry 1,500 rounds of 7.62mm ammunition. The pod weighs about 325 pounds fully loaded. Extensive use of reinforced honeycomb composites helps the system to attain this light weight.

The pod can be loaded with standard 7.62mm linked ammunition. The ammunition feed system is linkless, but a delinking loader is included in the pod. This allows support personnel to load the system without having to delink each round. When the gun system fires, the spent cartridge cases are ejected from the bottom of the pod.

The 7.62mm pod-mounted Gatlings are electrically driven. The pod contains the electric drive motor, a battery pack, and all control circuitry. The aircraft to which the system is mounted only needs to provide a firing signal and a trickle charge to keep the battery pack fully energized.

The GPU-5/A 30mm Lightweight Gun Pod

Chapter 11 discussed the GAU-8/A 30mm Avenger Gatling gun and the A-10 aircraft built around it. The 30mm GAU-8/A is the most powerful Gatling gun ever built, and the U.S. Air Force is quite pleased with its ability to defeat armored vehicles with its depleted uranium kinetic energy penetrator ammunition.

Based on this, General Electric developed a pod-mounted version of the GAU-8/A Gatling that extends the ability of other fighter and attack aircraft to engage armored targets. The resultant pod, the GPU-5/A, can be mounted on the A-4 Skyhawk, the A-7 Corsair, the

Figure 34 (top). The U.S. Army XM-18E1 7.62mm Gun Pod. The Air Force version is denoted as the SUU-11B/A. The system can fire at either 2,000 or 4,000 RPM (3,000 or 6,000 for the Air Force version).

Figure 35 (bottom). The GPU-5/A mounted on an F-5 Tiger. Note the centerline installation, which is preferred due to the system's aerodynamic drag and high recoil forces.

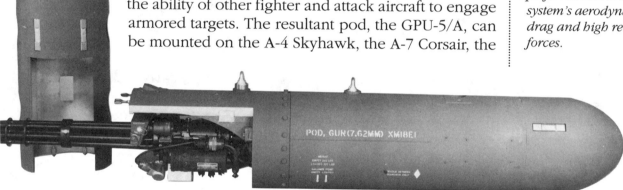

F-4 Phantom, the F-5 Tiger, the F-15 Eagle, the F-16 Falcon, the F-18 Hornet, the F-20 Tigershark, and the OV-10 Bronco. Figure 35 shows a GPU-5/A pod mounted on an F-5 Tiger.

The GPU-5/A system uses a four-barreled version of the Avenger Gatling gun denoted as the GAU-13/A (the GAU-8/A uses a seven-barreled gun). The GAU-13/A is pneumatically driven by a system that is fully contained in the pod. Its firing rate is 2,400 RPM. The GPU-5/A system can be mounted on either the centerline or wing stations (the centerline installation is preferred, however, due to the 30mm's high recoil forces). Fully loaded with 353 rounds of 30mm ammunition, the system weighs just over 1,900 pounds.

The 25mm GAU-12/U Gatling Gun

Another pod-mounted Gatling system that bears mention is the McDonnell Douglas Harrier AV-8B's 25mm GAU-12/U. Although this is not a classic pod-mounted system in the sense that it is not intended to be interchangeable from one aircraft to the next, nor does it mount on external weapons racks, the complete system is mounted in two pods beneath the AV-8B fuselage. One pod contains the ammunition storage system (which carries 300 rounds), while the other carries the 25mm Gatling gun and its pneumatic drive. A tunnel transports the ammunition from the ammunition pod to the gun pod. The two pods are further unique in that their aerodynamic structure actually provides additional lift to the aircraft.

15 Replica Gatling Guns

*T*he man carefully opened the crate. He had waited more than a year for this, the latest acquisition in his collection. He felt the excitement that comes from purchasing a thing of great quality and scarcity, something that one has to wait for no matter how much money is offered. As he gently removed the packing material, he saw that his wait (not to mention his $14,000) had been well worth it. The mahogany and polished metal Gatling gun was exquisite.

The story of the Gatling gun is truly amazing. As explained throughout this book, the weapon's history extends from the Civil War to today's modern weaponry. Modern Gatlings are used in all sorts of contemporary high-technology weapons systems: tank-killing aircraft, saturation fire cargo aircraft, tactical jet fighters, ships, and antiaircraft applications. All of this, to students of history and high-technology weaponry alike, is amazing. In a small town in Utah, however, something even more amazing is going on. Gatling guns true to the original designs of Dr. Gatling are being manufactured, and they're selling as quickly as they can be produced.

The Miniature Cannon Business

In 1961, a man named Karl Furr began a hobby he never dreamed would become a profitable enterprise. Out of a demand for fine craftsmanship and an appreciation for the weapons of a bygone era, he began making miniature cannon. Furr's products were recognized as unique and perfect replicas, and the Furr Arms business grew to include family, friends, and neighbors.

At first, Furr's primary product was a 1/6-scale James six-pounder cannon. These miniature cannon represent perfection, and anyone who has seen Furr's work will tell you that his company's products are simply exquisite. The James six-pounder cannon have solid brass barrels and black walnut carriages. They come equipped with miniature brass display balls, a ramrod, and the bucket and rope used to maintain the gun. Brass rims are heated and shrink-fitted to the fourteen-spoke walnut wheels. In recent

The Gatling
Gun: 19th
Century
Machine Gun
to 21st
Century
Vulcan

122

years, sixteen of Furr's 1/6-scale James cannon replicas have even been used to provide the cannon blasts in symphony orchestra performances of Tschaikovsky's *1812 Overture*.

The product line soon expanded to include other miniaturized cannon and a variety of Gatlings. Furr's cannon business grew, primarily as a result of the craftsmanship and perfection evident in his products. He soon offered 1/12-scale, 1/6-scale, and 1/3-scale models of the James cannon. These were followed by replicas of the 32-pounder lower-deck guns found on the HMS *Victory*. Both 1/10- and 1/3-scale versions (in brass or black walnut) are available.

The Gatling Challenge

In 1968, Karl Furr and a close associate, Paul Kuhni, were challenged by a customer to build a miniature Gatling gun. Their first project was a 1/3-scale Model 1883. This project held many challenges, not the least of which was converting the mechanism design from the centerfire .45/70 to the rimfire .22 cartridge. In succeeding years, the company added new versions of different miniaturized Gatling guns to its product line in several scales and calibers, ranging from a custom-made 1/6-scale .12-caliber version to a 3/4-scale model in the powerful .357 Magnum. Because Furr Arms has always emphasized attention to detail in every aspect of the guns it manufactures, production time can take as long as several hundred hours per gun. The firing mechanism is true to the original Gatling design, with the only changes being those necessary for the guns' reduced size and to handle different cartridges.

The Furr Arms factory is small, yet it has all of the machinery required to produce all of the parts necessary for the miniature Gatlings and the cannon replicas. Castings are designed in miniature from original Gatling guns (the Furrs cast these items in their own foundry). All brass parts are custom machined and polished to a high luster. Wooden parts receive five hand-rubbed coats of gun stock finishing oil.

Today the company manufactures a carriage-mounted Model 1883 (with ten barrels in an enclosed brass tube and an Accles feed), a tripod-mounted Model 1893 (with six barrels, also in an enclosed brass tube), a Model 1893 Police Gatling, a carriage-mounted Model 1874 Gatling (the company's most popular model, with ten exposed barrels and a Broadwell feed drum), and the latest edition, the Model 1876 Camel Gun. The guns are offered in several sizes, including 1/6-scale, 1/3-scale, 1/2-scale, and 3/4-scale. Specifications for the various Furr Arms replica Gatlings are shown in Tables 15-1 through 15-6.

Table 15-1
1/3-scale Model 1883 Gatling specifications
Height: 21"
Length: 35"
Caliber: .22 short
Width: 24"
Weight: 45 lbs.

Table 15-2
1/6-scale Model 1893 Gatling specifications
Height: 10"
Length: 8.5"
Caliber: .12
Width: 8.5"
Weight: 3.5 lbs.

Table 15-3
1/3-scale Model 1893 Gatling specifications
Height: 20"
Length: 17"
Caliber: .22 short
Width: 17"
Weight: 20 lbs.

Table 15-4
1/2-scale Model 1876 Gatling specifications
Height: 28"
Length: 34"
Caliber: .22 Long Rifle
Width: 31"
Weight: 78 lbs.

Table 15-5
1/3-scale Model 1874 Gatling specifications
Height: 21"
Length: 36"
Caliber: .22 short
Width: 24"
Weight: 45 lbs.

Table 15-6
1/6-Scale Model 1874 Gatling Specifications
Height: 10.5"
Length: 17.5"
Caliber: .12
Width: 12"
Weight: 5 lbs.

CONCLUSION The Future of the Gatling Gun

Although the pace of conventional weapons development has remained brisk, and other weapons systems (most notably the Chain Gun mentioned in Chapter 9) have made inroads into applications well-suited to the Gatling gun, it is unlikely that the Gatling gun will do anything other than evolve and continue to be found ideally suited for a variety of tactical weapons applications. A gun system concept that has survived for 130 years and sees current use on dozens of U.S. and allied weapons platforms is not going to disappear.

There are a variety of reasons the Gatling concept will survive, and Gatling guns will continue to arm new weapons platforms. The Gatling offers several inherent advantages over other single-barreled systems, including ultrahigh rates of fire and inherent reliability (if a round fails to fire in a Gatling, it is simply rotated through the action and cleared). The Gatling's high firing rate allows for covering a wide target area, which is something the single-barreled weapons cannot duplicate. Single-barreled weapons can make up for this with more precise shot placement, but to do so requires more sophisticated radar and other detection and targeting schemes. Such systems can work, but they necessarily entail much greater complexity, and with this comes reduced reliability and mission availability.

Emerging Technologies

New gun and ammunition developments will also make the Gatling gun more attractive in future weapons systems applications. Four promising new technologies are ring airfoil projectiles, monolithic grain propellants, case-telescoped ammunition, and gas guns.

Ring airfoil projectiles are basically projectiles shaped like toroidal wings (imagine an airplane wing wrapped around to form a doughnut, as shown in Figure 36). When a ring airfoil projectile spins and travels through the airstream, it generates lift.

Here's what's unique about ring airfoil projectile technology: as the projectile slows, its center of lift moves forward with respect to its center of mass. This has the effect of tilting the projectile slightly to the rear, which increases its lift. The projectile can be designed such that the velocity reduction is matched to the tilt-induced increase in lift.

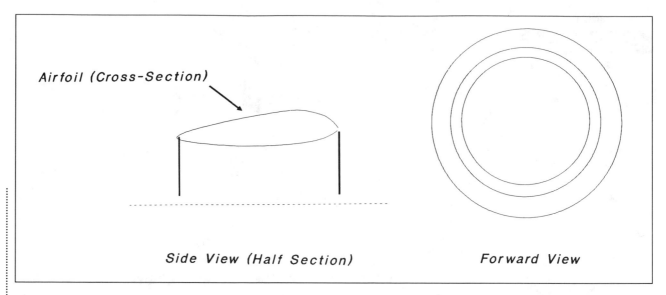

Airfoil (Cross-Section)

Side View (Half Section)

Forward View

The net effect is a trajectory that is very nearly flat and a tremendous increase in range. Ring airfoil projectiles can also be configured to carry a fuze and high explosive, offering great promise. As the ring airfoil projectile concept matures, it can only serve to make all gun systems (including the Gatling) more attractive.

Monolithic grain propellants offer an entirely new propellant concept (one that is more in line with solid propulsion rocket motors than conventional ammunition propellants). Instead of thousands of tiny powder granules in each cartridge case, the monolithic grain propellant has a solid ring of propellant material behind the projectile (much like a solid rocket motor). The concept is shown in Figure 37.

When a monolithic grain propellant cartridge is fired, the propellant has a more sustained burn rate than that of a conventional cartridge. The result is that instead of the projectile seeing a sharp pressure spike, it sees a sustained pressure for most of its travel through the gun barrel. With monolithic grain propellants, muzzle velocities in excess of 5,000 fps are possible (conventional muzzle velocities are typically in the 3,000 fps range). The increase in muzzle velocity will result in shorter times to the target and increased lethality (especially for kinetic energy kill mechanisms).

Cased-telescoped ammunition represents yet another new technology. The concept is shown in Figure 38. Instead of the more conventional ammunition configuration shown in Figure 37, the cased-telescoped round is a right circular cylinder. Prior to firing, the projectile is inside the cartridge case. When the round is fired, a precursor charge fires and pushes the projectile into the barrel. As soon as the projectile enters the barrel, the main propellant charge fires, completing the firing sequence.

The advantage of cased-telescoped ammunition is that it greatly

Figure 36. The ring airfoil projectile concept. This amazing new development adds both range and flatness of trajectory to projectiles and is ideally suited for Gatling gun applications. The projectile is a doughnutlike arrangement with a cross-section shaped like an airfoil. As the projectile slows, it tilts rearward, generating additional lift.

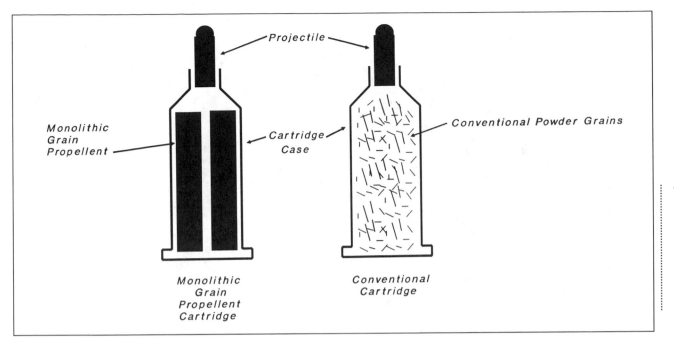

Projectile

Monolithic
Grain
Propellent

Cartridge
Case

Conventional Powder Grains

Monolithic
Grain
Propellent
Cartridge

Conventional
Cartridge

Figure 37. The monolithic grain propellant concept. Instead of numerous individual gunpowder grains, the monolithic grain concept has a single large grain with a passageway in the center. The single grain acts more like a rocket motor than conventional ammunition propellants, offering greatly increased muzzle velocity at sustainable barrel pressures. This and other ammunition developments assure the future of new gun systems, including the Gatling.

simplifies the ammunition storage and feed challenges associated with all gun systems and, in particular, with the feed and storage systems associated with high-rate-of-fire Gatlings. It's much easier to mechanically handle a simple cylinder than it is to cycle a conventional cartridge. Cased-telescoped ammunition also offers the potential for carrying larger quantities of ammunition. Most modern Gatling systems have ammunition capacity constraints that are driven by volumetric (rather than weight) considerations. General Electric, under contract with the U.S. Air Force, developed a fully operational 20mm Gatling gun using cased telescope ammunition. This gun system (referred to as the High Performance 20mm Cased-Telescoped Gun System) is shown in Figure 39. The high-performance gun has only half as many parts as the conventional M61A1 Vulcan cannon, and only one-third the number of moving parts. Ballistic improvements from the cased-telescoped ammunition double the gun system's projectile kinetic energy.

Gas guns represent another new technology that is already being applied experimentally to the Gatling. The concept involves a liquid or gas propellant being injected into a cylinder behind the projectile and then ignited to propel the warhead downrange. This simplifies the ammunition feed and storage even further (the system only has to handle projectiles instead of complete cartridges).

A Return to the Guns Versus Missiles Argument

In an earlier chapter we discussed the relative merits of guns versus missiles as aircraft armament for air combat fighters. This argument will likely continue. Future U.S. plans for aircraft armament are shrouded in secrecy on aircraft such as the F-117 Stealth fighter (which is believed not to have any gun system), the Air Force's Advanced Tactical Fighter, and the Navy's Advanced Tactical Aircraft.

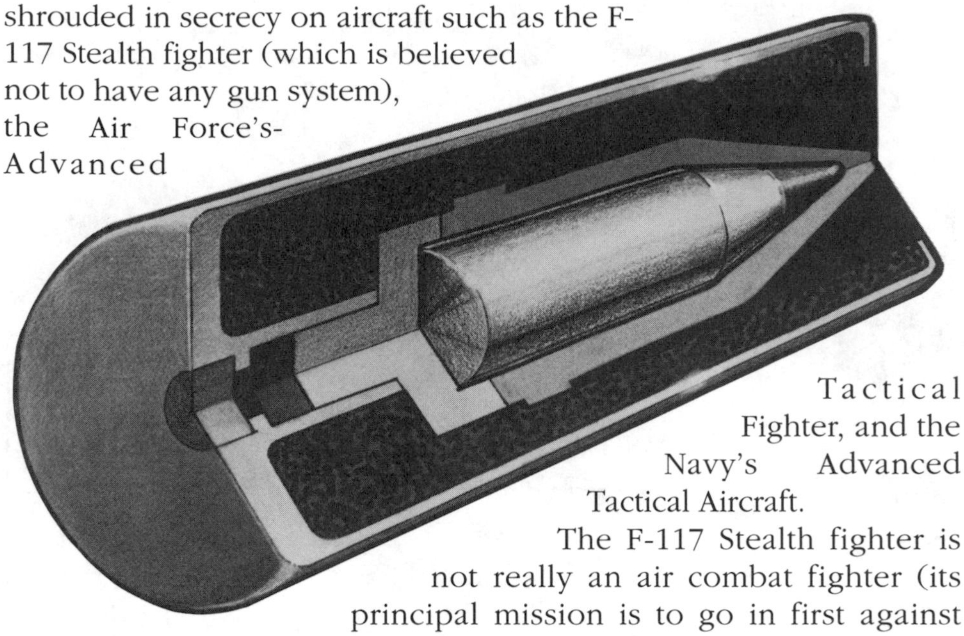

Figure 38. The cased-telescoped ammunition concept. The right circular cylinder configuration simplifies the ammunition feed and storage challenge, which promises increased ammunition payloads for future Gatling-based systems.

The F-117 Stealth fighter is not really an air combat fighter (its principal mission is to go in first against enemy air defense installations and defeat them to clear the way for other nonstealth aircraft). In a very real sense, the Stealth fighter is more like a mini-Stealth bomber (with an emphasis on tactical as opposed to strategic targets), and not an air-to-air combatant in the classic sense.

Air Defense

In the air defense role, the future of the Gatling is secure. The attempt to replace the Vulcan Air Defense System with the DIVAD (a non-Gatling-based gun system) ended dismally. Vulcan Air Defense Systems are still in service after defending forward area troops for a quarter of a century. New forward area air defense systems seem to center around combinations of either 25mm or 30mm Gatlings and a vehicle-based version of the Stinger antiaircraft missile. If the United States opts to replace its Vulcan Air Defense Systems, it is likely to do so with a system that includes a Gatling gun.

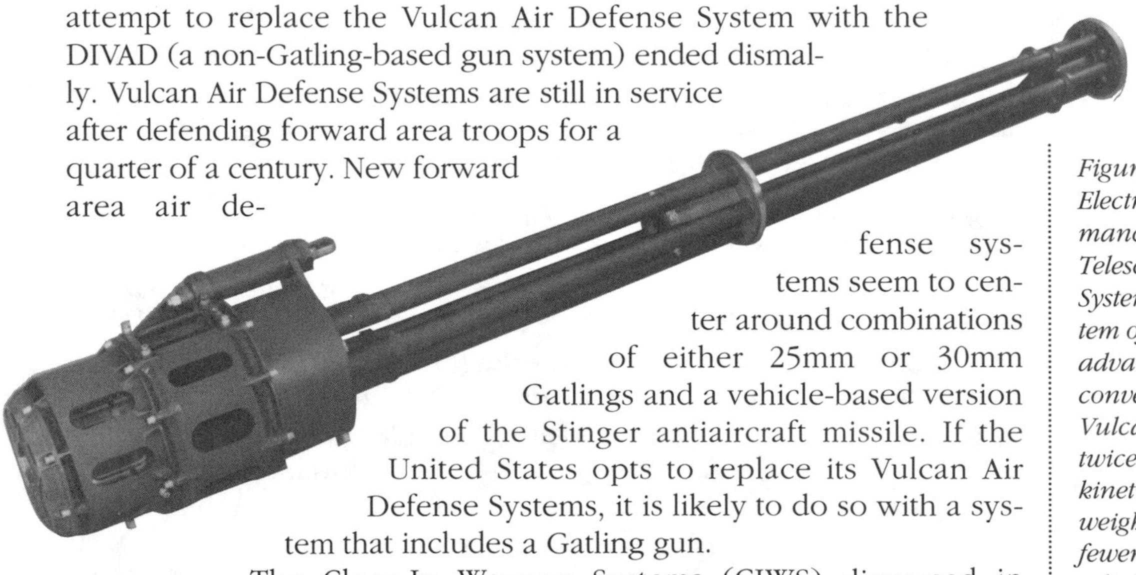

Figure 39. General Electric's High Performance 20mm Cased Telescoped Gun System. The new system offers numerous advantages over the conventional 20mm Vulcan, including twice the projectile kinetic energy, lighter weight, smaller size, fewer parts, increased reliability, simplified feed systems, and the potential to carry more ammunition in volume-constrained applications.

The Close-In Weapon Systems (CIWS) discussed in Chapter 13 will continue to evolve. For all their might, modern surface combat ships were essentially defenseless against sea-skimming antiship missiles until the Phalanx system was developed. The British Goalkeeper, a 30mm CIWS, will undoubtedly find new markets in other allied nations. Numerous studies have examined the feasibility of "upgunning" the U.S. 20mm Phalanx CIWS, and as the threat to shipping continues to evolve, it is likely that Phalanx will both find new markets and be retrofitted with new 25mm Gatlings.

•   •   •   •   •

This book has outlined the development of the Gatling gun from its inception during the Civil War to its current applications on a variety of modern combat systems. The Gatling gun concept has proven itself to be, in a very real sense, timeless. Future weapons systems will no doubt continue to apply the engineering elegance inherent to Dr. Gatling's design, assuring the survival of this most interesting weapons system and those values for which the United States stands.

129

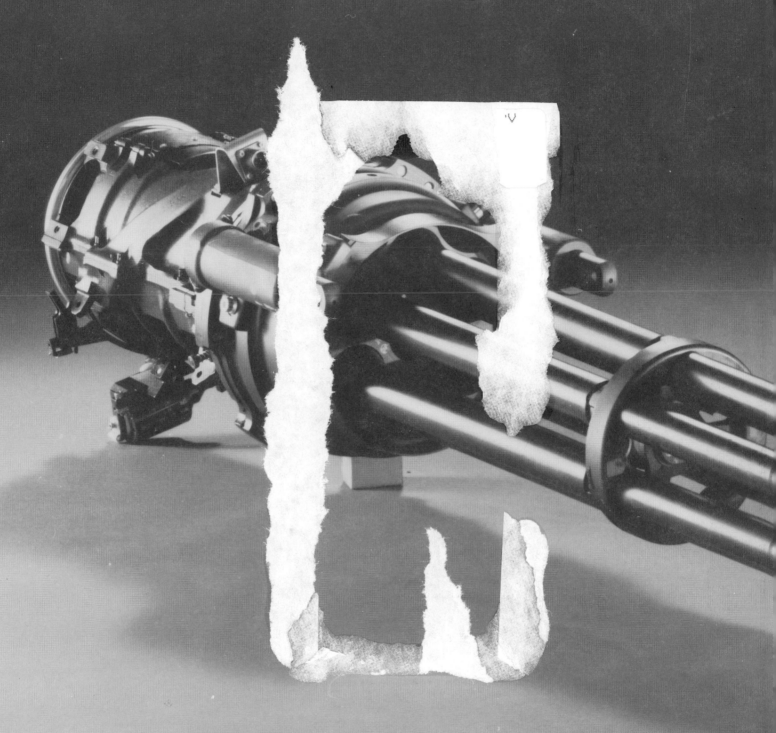